medical
oneness

the way to unite all forms of medicine

david nassim

Medical Oneness

Published by:
HI Publishing
Stone, Bucks
UK

www.healthinstinct.org
Copyright © 2010 by David Nassim
First published in 2011

ISBN :978-0-9566873-0-2

Editing by Nicky Ryde
Book Design, Illustration by Celine Hogan

medical oneness

For all who draw towards unity in healing

Acknowledgement

Thank you for the inspiration of this project from Jane, Mick and Lesley. Thank you to all those who I learned from because of their broad clarity, or their limitations and narrowness. All have benefited this project.

This work is impossible to be owned by an individual, it is a result of years of union with all the people I have met. Thank you dearly to Celine and Nicky for the book design and editing, without which this book could never have been possible.

Table of Contents

medical oneness

Introduction

We live in an age characterized by the global use of natural therapies - from the most ancient to the newest, from the subtlest to the most physical. As a therapist and a patient, I've witnessed outright aggression between one camp of medicine and another, each insisting that their way is the right way. Posturing has become the norm: "my way is better because it's more traditional"; "this one is the best because it's more results-orientated"; "my way works better than any other"; "I am an individual and this is "my" way of treating/teaching"; "I am self-sufficient as a practitioner". It is obvious of course that everyone, if seen as separate parts, is unique but Kofi Annan, Secretary-General of the United Nations, had this to say, in an article he wrote about contextualizing the individual and the possible way to "make things better".

> *"With only a click on a mouse people from different countries can talk to each other. An e-mail message can get from me to you in seconds, whether you live in the United*

States, Japan, Africa or South America....
Computers and modems help us to talk and
listen to each other across the world. But
it wouldn't do us much good if we didn't
already have a lot in common. And we do.
We may have a different religion, different
languages, different colored skins, but we
all belong to the human race. We all share
the same basic values."

It is the timeless truths, the universal principles, that bridge all time and place - or as Kofi Annan says "basic values" of Oneness.

Individualism and the belief in it, brings about the general fragmentation we see in modern medical-therapeutic practices which focus in separation, rather than wholeness. There is no-one to blame for this, modern medicine and therapeutic ideas are derived from the identification with a "self" within the human mind, as is all of society - its art, its science and its media. Actually natural medicine was meant to be a means out of this. Therefore Medicine is really something that is not to do with the individual, but yet is applied to seeming "individuals" by other seeming "individuals". Herein lies the conundrum: if medicine is required to be suited/tailored to the particular problem presented by the patient, while at the same time medicine is being expressed through the particularities of the practitioner, what room does this leave for unity? There has to be a base understanding which is common ground, where individual style is not the focus but is contextualized by healing itself through this uniqueness. This is not a negation of uniqueness but rather a realisation that this uniqueness cannot be owned and is a part of a large base, which allows us to follow Nature rather than attempt to take the reins. This book therefore aims to differentiate individualist stylism and root-principle. Over the last ten years, I have studied one of the most ancient of the natural medicines, that of Chinese medicine, to find what is at the root not just of this medicine but linking to all of healing. There is a plethora of individualistic approaches even within the breadth of Chinese medicine, but originally the ancient medicines of the various areas of the world, China being just one of them, were united in fundamental basic principles and were not focused on individualistic style. It is here we can contact basic natural principles, deeply embedded within ancient texts, which are universally applicable and allow natural medicine to once again be unified.

This book is not an attempt to force something, to try and push "my idea" onto all therapeutic professions so that they become one under "my direction". Actually, this has nothing to do with me, or anyone else, no teacher, lineage or doctrine can hold this. In fact, the universal principles involved in ancient medicine do not apply only to medicine or art or science or anything exclusionary - they are fundamental principles and do not require belief or enrollment into any specific construct. You need only to be human in order to make sense of them.

Natural principles are at the root of all our understanding, they are developed from our very instinctual senses. They are simply our directions back to sense or Centre, and as a result they form the backbone of all forms of medicine from the most subtle hands-off healing methods to the most physical and surgical forms. They are the principles of energy, the foundation of the idea of Oneness. I believe it is time for us to truly recognize this Oneness and re-introduce it to medicine and all other aspects of life, rather than allowing different branches of the same tree to become alienated from the roots. This book is an entry point for those who wish to do this.

The notion of this book is that if we go back far enough into our ancient heritage, mostly through ancient scripts and through those few still associated with a passed-on understanding of Oneness, or more rarely those who spontaneously utter this clarity in the modern day, or we look into the ways of life of indigenous peoples worldwide, there is a root underpinning all the ancient medical cultures - those of India, China, Greece, and others - that describes the energetic phases of life and is founded on the observation of unity in all things. In ancient cultures this formed the most basic of understandings and it was from there that natural medicine was coined and clarified. This was highly elucidated in ancient China, although this is not to negate the other regions of the world. Ancient China, however, gives us principles that are so raw, pure and succinct that they can easily be applied to anything. This gives us the bare essentials, the philosophy of non-dualism in its most unhampered form. The bulk of this material was written from about 500 BC to AD 150, and during this time medicine developed to understand and explain shamanic practices and expression in a non-belief, an almost modern scientific approach of empiricism which we could call "pure" empiricism or "pure" science; this will be explained further later. The foundational principles of Chinese medicine are therefore the same as those of Indian and Greek medicine, if seen with a mind open to unity. It is here that we need to start to form a foundational, energetic structure that can underpin the myriad expressions of natural medicine on offer today, the ancient principles being like the background that holds all the parts of the foreground. The motivation for doing this is that if there was such a thing as a universal diagnostic language, then therapists would no longer attempt to "know everything". Instead, their focus could be on knowing their own healing expression relative to and contextualized by others and on joining with other therapists who expressed themselves differently, all using the same language of diagnosis. Instead of the discipline or theory, or focusing on the tool of treatment being the healer (e.g. acupuncturist, herbalist, osteopath), it would be about what the person is as a natural expression and personality, as an instrument in and of nature, and how they were treating, they wouldn't need a label. The tool of treatment is merely an expression of the therapist, rather than the other way around, which means in fact, that everyone has a different style of expression, a unique place in the spectrum of healing, but this only makes sense in context of a universal principle. In exactly the same way, we look into the ancient idea which was understood in modern times by Carl Jung amongst others, as the "Collective-unconscious" or more fully the "Super-Conscious" or Oneness, underpinning the "self". This allows for uniqueness but also clearly recognizes that what looks like an "individual" isn't, and as such we become cells within the whole body of a united expression. The music score is the same but we all have different voices.

The separation of natural medicine starts with the label of our profession. Practitioners of natural medicine all have the same focus, namely holism, yet when it comes to referring someone to another practitioner, there is such a lack of understanding about what other practitioners do, what his/her discipline is useful for and what it isn't, because the practitioner is hidden behind a label. It is a kind of non-sense of sifting through marketed material and often limited modern theoretical ideas, rather than the recognition of healing-quality that leads to the right therapist finding the right patient and vice-versa. If we understood that we are all fingers on the same hand, and if we spoke the same basic language, the process of making suitable referrals to the right practitioner would become so much clearer, thereby expediting the process of healing. It would also acknowledge the differences in the varied expressions of natural medicine. A universal language, however, requires some agreement. It requires us to acknowledge that there is, in fact, a problem and that it would be wise for us to speak to one another in universal terms. It requires that we see ourselves as One, a recognition of the fact that all humans are cells in the same body. We need to understand that working in isolation ends harmony, it doesn't induce it. We need to consider why balance can only be found when those who are grounded and practical are met by those who are inspirational. We need to honestly express what it is that we really are, rather than attempting to be that which we are not, or are labelled as. If we had a background of a foundational language with which to express ourselves, it would change natural medicine, it would allow any tool to be used to its fullest - and to be used appropriately. Therefore it is at the theoretical base level rather than theoretical "principles of life" level with which we all need to be aligned. The tools in many ways are very similar: herbs, needles, specialist lasers, scalpels, even hands themselves (usually they have 5 fingers!) - they are all objects which become extensions of healing. Sometimes tools and "things" are not involved in the therapy at all and it is simply the healer and patient, which makes it easier to see through to the nature that this is purely "healing". But even here, in the modern world, people will label and sell their "way" with all sorts of trademarked methods, making a something out of a no-thing. To be unified at the theory-principle base level would truly be an opening into a new age, rather than the modern age, which is what we have created - the true "new age" has yet to be born.

You may be thinking: how would this author know about homeopathy, naturopathy, or any of the other expressions of medicine on offer today - when he has studied Oriental medicine? Others within Oriental medicine might say that I appear to be speaking of a "style" of practice which seems to be eclectic rather than specific, and that this is a style in itself! A stylistic label can only be claimed if a person is coming from a "position", a point that is fixed, a view or an "angle", not the underpinning or overall view that incorporates all views. This cannot be called a style - it is what everyone agrees on within each style. If the common ground is understood then this forms a base for people to directly follow a personal style of expression unhampered, one could call it a universal underpinning theory. The key point of this book is not to focus in gaining knowledge of all theoretical styles so that the reader can become the "king/queen of therapies", it's about acknowledging and accepting all of them and contextualizing them within the principles of wholeness at their very roots - their universal language. The theoretical styles of modern medicine, science-based or not, are generally limited due to the nature of them being born from modern times. We must stop looking at modern theory or tools themselves to define us and instead look beneath this, into the depths of the foundational principles of each form of medicine. We must consider how, if we look at the energetic basis to the medicine, we would be able to communicate with other therapeutic traditions and not fear losing our world-view for theirs. How could we "lose" anything if we are coming from the same Oneness at root? Our foundations would be unified and our diagnostics would read the same, perhaps speaking in different dialects but all are the languages of the common-tongue of Oneness, not of modern separatist idealism, however different our techniques are at resolving the problem. This also introduces the understanding of the limitation of ourselves and how we fit into the whole, rather than attempting to be all of the whole, self-contained and separated-off, playing to strengths rather than hiding weaknesses and extending outwards to other people to support the "weaknesses" which are in fact our larger body: humanity. The problem with modern individualistic or personal ideas associated with medicine is that they often believe that they are the whole within themselves, and as a result they cannot see the blind-spot of their expression which limits their practice and forms a clique. It is the people who sense Oneness, i.e. who can see the whole picture, who then can see that their strand of expression is part of something larger. This then naturally looks to unite with, rather than segregate off from, as it is obvious that the basic premises of a therapy/theory built from the individual's expression alone will only be of use to the individual, and will not allow for another person being taught it to necessarily find their own style on a larger common ground. It's the same as social understanding, if we consider all people as One at root, then there is acceptance, whatever those people may look like or the various expressions they have or where they come from in the world. Anything else is a form of racism!

There are of course theorists and thinkers who have ideas and then attempt to manipulate reality into these concepts. This is why we need to go back to the ancient material. Old is not better, but still has an intuitive sense and generations of accumulated understanding, it is consensus, not individual-based, it is instinctive and this is why it's useful - it underpins. Ancient China produced numerous theories and ideas and manipulations of such work (usually after AD 200, for example, dominant Confucian idealism), but there is a lineage of those who still use senses, rather than painting by numbers. These people hark back to a time when humans were one with nature and needed no formula to know something intuitively. It is from here that the principles of medicine come, and so are not theoretical but intuitive and sensory information, from observation. This is the thread we have left, of our way back home to Eden.

What I envision and what this book is about is a situation where

all practitioners of natural medicine acknowledge a background
- an energetic heritage by which they diagnose the patient, be
it psychological or physiological or anything else. Then, from
this place, they are able to understand and work with other
practitioners to create health care that is not only exactly what
is needed, but is efficiently, sustainably executed and in union
with the patient, not confusing them or taking them into realms
of complication that add to their anxiety. I envision a situation
where all practitioners see the Oneness underneath it all, and
operate from that perspective. If practitioners are complex, their
patients will be as well. If our minds as practitioners are filled
with hierarchy, theory, dead-ends and separation, this is passed
directly on to patients. The natural therapist, or the person
drawn to healing because it is what they are, (outside of ideas
of hierarchy, personal power or control mentality which is not
really the realm of the medicine, but rather sickness), go towards
this because it is closer to an at-one-with-life sense; why should
this then stop at the personal interaction with a patient and
personal ideas about medicine and personal judgments about it?
Should it not be that medicine is a whole movement, rather than
based on the ideas of individuals? This is a call for union, and I
offer the ancient track to a universal language with which to do
this in a complete way. This is not a perfect model, but the only
imperfection is my own expression of it. Within what will be
said in this book are the threads to an understanding which is as
relevant today as it is ancient, as universal as it is Chinese, and
as dissolving of boundaries as it is of allowing unique expression,
anchored in Oneness. To you, my fellow therapist, I suggest you
might consider the following as a background to what you already
do, requiring you to make no intentional change, but allowing
the possibility for you to see differently, whatever your style of
practice or theory, and perhaps allowing you to speak to other
practitioners, in order that we may join together in groups which

may eventually extend like seas, to see that natural medicine really means Oneness medicine, and that medicine is Oneness.

chapter one

The way it is now - and why: mind-identity and separation

Before launching into reasons for investigating and forming a universal background for practitioners of natural medicine, we must first be in agreement about the source of the problem with which we are dealing. In ancient expression, "energy" is everything in the universe, it is absolutely everything that is. This is a sea of energy, a totally unified field that has been expressed as such by mystics and physicists alike. This is the first premise we start with, simply Oneness, a point that is very easy to agree with in fact. If we are in acknowledgement of holism, then we have to start with the obvious - acknowledging that "we" are actually not a "we" or separate parts, but an indivisible whole. Therefore when I say "I", in true terms it means "I am that I am," rather than "I am David" or "I am Bob" or "I am Joan." I will assume, therefore, that we are in agreement about the first premise. Secondly, we must clearly understand dis-ease, which is what we are all involved with, to be a lack of acceptance of or a resistance to the notion (thought and theory) and the actuality (sense/instinct or

11

intuition) of Oneness. To some degree, we all experience suffering whenever there is an idea of "me" or "you" as being utterly apart. The ancients called this sufferance which is another term for dis-ease. Pain is very different from sufferance or dis-ease. Pain is an actual phenomenon, it is a pathological process of change associated with pain reception and energy blockage. However, pain is utterly in tune with natural phenomena - it is a sign or symptom. Pain therefore cannot be cured. Suffering, however, can be, or at least acknowledged, which essentially means a move towards "cure", and that was the original foundation of medicine. The process of allowing the body to relax from a state of tension and contraction to a state of expansion and relaxation is the movement we see every day in clinical situations, which is the alleviation of the idea of a separate, individuated self and a realization, however this may occur, of Oneness. This is curative. So a patient can be cured and still be in pain. This will be clear for those of you working with terminally ill patients and those in trauma wards. The pain can of course be heavily increased by suffering or identification with the idea of pain. This can magnify pain to the point of death, it can exaggerate pathological change and increase pain, as the pain is focused-on and energy contracts more heavily around the site of injury or pathology. However, levels of pain reduce as suffering reduces, always to levels that are appropriate to the injury/issue.

When we talk about "curative" in natural medicine, we mean curative in the sense of the root of the problem. Curing pain is curative of the "branch" problem, not the "root" problem, or its fundamental core, so we can't really call it curative at all. This is because once this symptom is resolved, another will manifest elsewhere, which is what we constantly see with the effects and "side effects" of bio-medical intervention. The root is sufferance, the branch is pain. The root is the origin of the dis-ease within the patient's identification with a pain or problem. The branch is the local area or symptom of this, in the form of pain. The less we look at the root, the more the pain will increase, and so the greater the need for medicine to deal with the acute issues. The greater the acknowledgment of the suffering, the less pain there is and the less need for aggressive medical intervention. Suffering seems intangible and "unreal" to those who require it to be a physical issue; pain, on the other hand, is almost measurable and is often thought of as more "real" by modern bio-medicine. Pain is easier to see, as it is at the periphery of something, whereas suffering is going on at the heart of it, within the core of the person. That is why there is often a gap in understanding for those within modern fragmented concepts. Please realize when I say "fragmented" this is not a criticism, it's looking at the concept from a view of the whole of something, not that "I can see this and no-one else can". In fact I'm taking the broad view which is the majority view, that of all people and all of nature, not the minority position, the modern scientist or individualist perspective, which is obviously narrowed, but of the place that this scientism looks from, a pure-observational non-analytic viewing - this is no special idea, it's simply as it is, the background context.

Mind-identification is the dis-ease itself. I use this term to mean the pathologic-psychology informing the physiology or simply mental-emotional suffering; this is what is meant here by mind-identity and mind-identity means dis-ease. Resolving this is curative, because this is the absolute base - from here pain is reduced and most symptoms fade for good. When we treat pain we focus on the symptoms, when we see suffering, we acknowledge the whole person and the context of life itself. If natural therapists recognize this as the second premise of our investigation, then we are in agreement for the remainder of this book.

Medicine developed from the ancient shamanic expression in connection with an increasing anxiety about death, which was the first sign of beginnings of the idea of "separateness" in human beings, the belief in being separate from the world as mankind continued its growth. As anxiety grew, the field of medicine grew right alongside it in an attempt to counter this expansive, mind-identified, suffering-based issue. With the passage of time, we have lost track of the ancient realization that suffering is the foundation which needs to be acknowledged; instead, we focus on pain. In bio-medicine pain is the prime focus, greater than any other. Dis-ease spreads very easily, as humans are not separate beings. Since we are One and there is no separate individual, the collective mind-identity of humanity is interlinked in its suffering. Ideas within medicine such as the "cure me/fix-me" mentality ignore the reality of this Oneness. The idea is firstly that there is something "wrong" which needs fixing. Actually, medicine is not really about this. What natural medicine understands to be curative is the ending of the idea that there is a separate person to fix; it means that the pain or problem is contextualized by a relaxation into a non-ownership of the pain. This is not denial but a realization that pain occurs, although it is not happening to an individuated person. The pain is simply occurring, without reason or judgment. It is as it is. This realization is curative. Saying "Fix me!" stems from the idea that you can be fixed by doctors focusing on the pain, the symptoms, and the branches of the problem. Though patients often start out believing that this is possible, the illusion doesn't last long. There might be great belief in the doctor, who due to their own notion of separation will feed a hierarchical mentality that sets them apart as a "higher being", and this does affect the body and allow change. However it also creates a doctor to patient hierarchy, the patient doesn't see the healing as a unity and as a result if symptoms develop again, which they will without the doctor, the faith in the doctor will also die, and then the problems will return and stay until another therapist arrives on the scene. This is not the idea of self-healing, in that the "self" is the dis-ease, so often medicine really is about getting to the point of letting-go/relaxation where nature can do the healing. From Voltaire:-

"The art of medicine consists in amusing the patient while nature effects the cure".

Specialization is innate within us. As practitioners, we have a specific expression in the world and tend to have a singular focus. If we come from this point of view only, to the exclusion of the background context, we lose perspective about what we are doing and end up prescribing inappropriate treatments. Say, for example, we are built like a sledgehammer, we then practise like a sledgehammer, understanding that a sledgehammer is the appropriate tool for pounding nails into planks of wood. Yet, if we use this same sledgehammer approach on an eggshell, the results would be disastrous. When this happens, the practitioner is seeing only himself and his practice - he uses the same approach with everything. This is the problem of modern medicine, due to the lack of background sensitivity and foundation principles everyone gets the sledgehammer approach.

It is important to be specialize, to understand and accept our specialty in relation to particular symptoms, patients, and tools of practice, but at the same time it is critical to understand the unifying objective situation, which sometimes necessitates a referral to other practitioners. This is about self-understanding more than anything else. Modern medicine is excellent at specialization in symptoms, but it is very limited at seeing the big picture on a general basis. This means that we really need all specialists to be rooted in "general practice" as well, rather than just focused on their specialty. This general practice must be founded on general principles, rather than in response to symptoms. It is these general principles that have been lost and will be discussed here.

What this book tries to explore is the branch in relation to the root. As practitioners, we are all leaves and branches, but some of us are aware of being connected to the root while others of us are not. Those who sense the connection to the root have a broader perspective, they don't get caught up in the details of what they are doing. Those who believe they are just the leaves and branches tend to become egoists and apply subjective logic to everything. In modern bio-medicine what is called, "general practice" is incredibly specialized, as anyone who has been to the doctor will know. The problem of specialization is that a doctor's mind is being drawn inward, trained to focus on small parts separate from each other, rather than seeing the part within the whole. The art of seeing the part in the whole includes noting the background as well as the foreground. This is the basis of holistic medicine, but is often considered "too vague" or "too uncertain" by the practitioners of an individualistic style or bio-medicine. In fact, the certainty and accuracy is within the broader viewing angle. Without this, it results in a dentist looking only at teeth and a gum specialist looking only at the gums. Ancient doctors may have been good at treating a particular symptom of dis-ease from the particular region they were in, because its occurrence was regular, influenced by climate; yet they would not have called themselves "specialists," because they were always contextualizing the patient's problem and seeing the whole picture, treating the root as well as the manifesting disease symptom. Consider a modern example - "infertility" is a specialization today, and practices specializing in this are often found within big city areas. The key issue should be why infertility is happening in the big city, rather than just how to help these people with infertility problems to become pregnant within this environment. One is attempting to force nature's hand here and this is one of the reasons why focusing only on the symptoms of dis-ease is inappropriate, in all cases. Natural medicine developed from this origin of Oneness, so we must acknowledge this in ourselves and in our consideration of holism. If there is holism, then nothing can be separate from it, nothing can be detached from the great sea of energy which we are.

Therefore dis-ease is only the *idea*, which is a physical or visceral experience, intertwined with the mind - this body experience we can call emotion. By emotion, I mean physical pain brought on by inner conflict/sense of separation, inner anger, and anxiety at a deep level - general angst. These, as well as the mental ideas and pictures derived from these feelings which may also trigger these states, are one and the same thing. Emotion is therefore a more physical form of mind-identity. The identification of a person as being the contents of memories in the mind or feelings in the body is bound to lead to suffering because these things change and move with the tide, constantly threatening the end of "what I thought I was." This is the foundation of dis-ease, our heritage passed on from generation to generation, with natural mind expansion and upward movement of energy (heat rising), due to our natural standing upright position, which is a totally natural phenomenon but one that has created dis-ease, and with it medicine, to counter this process and bring us down to earth again. Everything is natural, including that which we consider to be un-natural, but usually when we use the word "un-naturalness" it means "brought about by the notion of separateness" and that's what makes us look at and sense it differently from those things formed by wild nature itself. Medicine is always a return to the wild, to the instinctual nature of things, and is a movement away from separateness. This is not to negate the function and use of the mind and its ability to analyze and understand and imagine, but it is to recognise that these images, ideas and memories are not "what is absolute and all". They are more like clouds in the sky, they come and go on the background canvas of Oneness, which is the true nature of what all of life is part of, like a jellyfish with myriad tentacles. The mind is contextualized and so is seen for what it is, and no longer identifies with itself; this is the end of "self" and the return to Oneness.

I must also add that there is no positive or negative, good or bad associated with emotions or mind-identity. To clarify, the word "emotion" means from Latin "emovere" - "move out, disturb, agitate"; the nature of emotion is therefore not good or bad but is a disruption in the flow of life and this is not to do with health. If we want to consider what it does: mental-emotional patterns increase suffering and without them suffering is reduced. That is all. All emotion is associated with this. Love, bliss, expansion, joy, and a sense of peace are not emotions; all of these are beyond duality. They are behind everything and are other words for Oneness, really the point when duality, belief in separation, ends. Hence, instead of looking at positive and negative, it is best to consider mental-emotion as the foreground of a picture and the background as joy/ peace/love, etc.

When we focus on the foreground we may not notice the background, even though it is constantly present. Suffering is always a contraction of mind-identity, it is a binding of the energy of the body forming mental illusion and bodily emotion. Openness is health. Please understand that contraction is a warped aspect of life (yang) energy which would normally be open. When suffering/dis-ease is present there is a resistance of the flow of natural energy due to an imagined separate sense of self at the base of all movements in life, forming vicious cycles of a repetitive process of existence which occur to breaking point or a ripeness when they can be resolved. Healing can only occur when it is the right time, this too was understood by the ancients.

I will now continue with this investigation, with the above firmly fixed in our consciousness: that Oneness is our root, and that separation is the idea of brokenness from our root, and is, in fact, an illusion. When Oneness is recognized, our name drops away and we no longer have a person in here (pointing towards myself), who we can call "David," "Bob," or "Joan." Oneness is always in the background, forever carrying us, forever the ocean of which we are a single wave. If this is acknowledged and agreed upon, then the rest of this book is child's play to understand. Consider the poem below. If we can see that "I" is the egoic illusion, and "the Lord" is Oneness, *inclusive* of the illusion, then this picture is complete.

"Footprints"
by Mary Stevenson 1936

One night I dreamed I was walking along
the beach with the Lord.
Many scenes from my life flashed across the sky.
In each scene I noticed footprints in the sand.
Sometimes there were two sets of footprints,
Other times there were one set of footprints.

This bothered me because I noticed
that during the low periods of my life,
when I was suffering from
anguish, sorrow or defeat,
I could see only one set of footprints.

So I said to the Lord,
"You promised me Lord,
that if I followed you,
you would walk with me always.
But I have noticed that during the most trying
periods of my life
there have only been one set of footprints
in the sand.
Why, when I needed you most, have you not
been there for me?"

The Lord replied,
"The times when you have seen only one set of
footprints in the sand,
is when I carried you."

(source :- www.wowzone.com/fprints.htm)

chapter 2

Differentiating style from principle

For me, the key issue that barred my view of a spectrum of medicine as one light was the idea of style. It initiated my interest into Shiatsu, which, at the time I was studying it, had three or four different variations and styles, all of which were taught to us so that we would have a "broad base." However, this only created confusion for the practitioner and then for the patient as a result - you reap what you sow! This led me to seek out the root of Oriental medicine, which I found to be the same root as all medicine in the process. To clarify some terms I will use: a style is the expression of one or a group of practitioners, adhering to one idea, which allows this group to investigate the human body in a particular way, often using a specific tool or tools to do so. A principle is something that underlies the style which is universal to all styles. If understood, a principle allows one to use any tool to effect change, adapting to different people's climatic location and situation, rather than looking at just the stylistic theory and its tools as the limitation of what can be done. A principle is totally unlimited, a style is limited to a particular practitioner or group. Focusing on a style can often be about separating off – for example from other styles -and about investment in individualism. A principle attempts to see the big picture and contextualize styles within a spectrum of understanding. We need to acknowledge our unique expression, but only based in the universality of principles; we need to look at what we are doing contextually, or we will be lost in subjectivity. If we all work in stylistic modalities medicine will never be unified and the constant debate about intricacies of practice will continue, namely "you do this, and I do that" and "my way is better than your way." The goal becomes supremacy, or at the very least, an ambivalence towards others.

This has nothing to do with the universal premises we have already agreed upon above, Oneness and the understanding of dis-ease as separation. We could say that ideology based in stylistic ideas actually imparts to the patient the notion of individualism, which *is* dis-ease, or separation from the whole, so it perpetuates the same old thing. If we step away from style and look at principle we can find the needle in the context of the haystack. This is an entirely different approach from those we have today, a deeply old way of looking at one another and the world. Instead of seeing the differences, which are naturally going to be created anyway, our eyes need to be set on unity.

Every diagram and system of number and every combination of harmony, and revolution of the stars, must be made manifest as the "One Through All" to him who learns in the proper way. And it will be made manifest, as we say, "a man learns by keeping his gaze on Unity."

- from Plato's work, Timaeus
(quoted in: Harvey C. & S., 1999)

medical oneness

chapter 3

Fragments within Oneness: ancient principles of natural medicine differentiated from modern "natural" medicine

When looking at the ancient understanding of the energetic Oneness sea, we must also note how modern Western ideas of natural therapy and natural ideology fit into this picture. Here we have to consider modern science differentiated from ancient principles. In fact, because ancient principles are non-dualist, they are also non-judgmental; this means that there is no good or bad, all is accepted. Modern Western medicine and science and all its ideas and philosophy are happily swallowed by the wholeness of Oneness. They are the background, the board on which the jigsaw puzzle is being constructed. The whole is the whole, so it doesn't negate the parts, but recognizes them all as part of something bigger; it fills in the gaps, so to speak. Modern science is made up of fragments. I should clarify that when I say "ancient," it means something very particular. There was no

"Golden Age" of humankind in the past which I am idealizing. People have been involved in the suffering of individualism for 100,000 years or so, evolving gradually from the dawn of standing upright (*Homo erectus* 1.8-1.5 million years BC). However, there have been those who have known the root back to sense, who have had the "health instinct", as one might call it. It is these that I am referring to and the expressions in the ancient material which can still be found in those people who have indigenous background, untouched by civilization or at least little affected by it. Today this understanding is hugely eclipsed by modern individualists, but then nature, which is the foundation of the health-instinct, is far, far larger than the modern world. Within the modern however there is connection, a passing on of the message of these ancient people's wisdom which still remains, although dwindling.

It is interesting how, all over the world at around the same time, recognition of something important occurs. Buddha in India, Lau Tzu in China and Parmenides in Greece were all people with the same vision, because they are all one expression, a wave of clarity from their past, if you will. This, too, is occurring today and it is reconnecting with this sense, like an echo. The connection with these people - the originators of essential messages of Oneness - is where medicine stemmed from, before it was corrupted by individuals again. Just prior to this wave also was separatism, although not on the scale we see it today in the modern world. These waves seem to recur at different critical points in time from the origin of the "problem" and our belief that we have lost an Eden which is in fact constantly present. It is a wave of ripeness to move to simplicity once again, a calling-home to the simple, when things have become too complex within mind-identity. In our time too this wave is re-occurring with more and more people speaking about the return to Oneness and simplicity. This is the "ancient" connection spoken about here.

Considering this allows us to start with a clear differentiation in our quest for a universal background and Oneness. There is nothing original. This is deeply true because in the modern mentality we feel we are in an upward evolving process to get somewhere, but there is in fact nothing to "get" or "achieve" and this is the process of the mind-identity itself trying to "get somewhere" (home in fact!) - it is the dis-ease. Hence when we are looking at almost all modern ideas of medicine, those which are not inclusive of the ancient clarity, or which ignore it for a "modern" "new" or "updated" system of modern times these will be met with the difficulty that those systems will be inclusive for all people but will likely be very much associated with the ideas and mentality of the originator him/ her self. It's not about originality or uniqueness in the understanding of medicine, it's about knowing we are all human and while we are all unique the dis-ease itself is something only humans carry, no other animal has this problem.

Aspects of medicine derived from a Western science model or modern fragmentary mind-set begin with a base which is not grounded in ancient instinctual understanding. It is non-energetic in base and this generally means that there are more aspects for these people to consider, in order to ground themselves in an energetic unity. Numerous examples are mentioned in this book (please see chapter 6). All of these forms and others are from a theoretic ideology presented on a mechanistic and/or physical basis, not having a full picture of the notion of the energetic which they reach out toward, for example, the direction of modern quantum physics, which starts to look like the ancient understanding but is as yet still stuck in mechanistic logic.

On the other hand, practitioners of energy-based medicines will have little struggle understanding what I am talking about here. Reiki practitioners, acupuncturists, energy workers of all kinds, spiritual healers and psychotherapists of the more eclectic and spiritual rather than mind-base, intuitive healers - all of these people have developed a sensitivity to some degree and know of the Oneness, though are often seen as more "flaky" by modern ideologies. Actually, these people are connecting to a deeper sense of reality or are moving towards the ancient or indigenous/ instinctive/natural fundamentals of healing. Oriental medicine, Ayurvedic medicine, ancient Greek medicine, Mayan, Incan and shamanic medicines, all fall into this category and are the ancient roots of medicine worldwide - they are global medicine's roots. The difficulty that the Western modern medicine or modern mind-based therapies have is they are attempting to join with the energetic, without wholly letting go of the physical and the "real", in terms of mechanistic models of the way things seem. Even though they may know of the ideas of modern physics and its yet to be "discovered" understanding of unified field theory, this enquiry has also reached the biological sciences, which along with physics, at their cutting edge are using mechanistic Newtonian thinking. Ideas like biological fields known as morphogenic fields, bio-resonance, psycho-neuro-immunology, also being called mind-body medicine and related work into epi-genetics, are arenas which are squashed into a zone where therapies resulting from are neither energetic-based nor interested in the purely mechanistic. Until physics sees the bigger picture all science is stuck with this. The individuals who are proponents of these movements and therapies forming from them are not accepted by standard modern bio-medicine as "legitimate" or "usable" and are often considered by energy-medicine as limited. This overlooks their brilliance. These people are making a transition, and as a result they are more inspired

28

than most of the mainstream medical profession, who would prefer not to embrace a unified understanding as it would shake their worldview to its roots. The "new biology/medicine" is making a public move towards acknowledging dis-ease, rather than advocating the focus on anti-pain or numbing medication.

However, for those interested in this transition field, I would suggest that although the ideas in this book may be somewhat challenging, this book is actually written for you. You have fewer ideas and boundaries around a style than energy medicine practitioners do, you have less resistance to letting go of your "master's" approach and there is more possibility for you to see and feel for yourselves what is true in the following expression of the ancient principles of energetic Oneness. You are more likely to be able to found yourselves in a sense of connectedness with these principles and avoid the pitfalls of separating yourselves within an art. This unfortunately is the plight of the practitioners of energy medicine who attempt to sell their own brand of connection to the highest bidder, or have the pretence of a hierarchical lineage and power to uphold to students and patients alike. This imparts the very same consciousness with it, that of separation. What *is* can be seen on the surface and to its depth. There is even truth in a lie, consider the chameleon: we say it is "camouflaged, hiding its true colour," when in fact, the truth is that it is the colour it is, now. One needs to be aware of these things when finding a teacher or theory of practising.

When speaking the language of modern Western culture and medicine we are speaking the language of fragmentation: white cells are separate from red cells, the liver and heart are of not one but separate organ systems. In ancient understanding, it is the energetic Oneness, the sea of energy, which pervades everything. The whole person, in its total form, is everything and the whole of anything can only ever be everything. This concept is not difficult, it is just beyond the normal ways we think. In "normal" terms, which are quite abnormal in comparison with the laws of the rest of the universe, we consider our bodies to end at our skin and so are constantly in defence of this border, causing profound suffering due to a belief in separation; separation requires defence of the individual. Our bodies, however, do not end at our skin. This is of course is recognized by the search for a unified theory of physics. The Gaia Theory from James Lovelock's brilliant vision of a unified scientific naturalism, expressing global unity of biological connection, is only now thirty years since its investigation, becoming truly and fully recognised as a possibility by scientists. (BBC - Beautiful Minds documentary, 2010). This surely bolsters the aim of the quantum model as being the prime field from which all life in the universe originates. As a result, when we refer to "Modern" Western medicine, we are expressing something cut off from the whole, no matter what it is. In natural medicine, when we report a body issue we mean this in connection with everything else and all such things that resonate with this aspect. For example, in Western medicine the liver means the oblong organ below the diaphragm and lungs, on the right side of the body. In natural medicine, the liver organ is also the energetic of Spring within the body, it resonates with the colour green, with the muscles of the body, and with an energetic pathway that affects an outwardly-moving dynamic physical expression.

This too resonates with the energetic quality in all things. Not only that, but when you effect change in this expression in a single person, this effects change throughout existence, so there is never a time when one is away from wholeness. The idea of pulling away from the ancient rather than seeing it as a basis and instinctual heritage is part of the mind-identity pulling up and outwards, it is part of the dis-ease. Tradition and dogmatism are not the focus here but rather the pure observation of senses which runs like a thread through the ancient material, this is our human heritage. Modern culture, language and ideas are not wrong but they are fragmented and therefore part of the dis-ease process. The language of medicine therefore must be different, based in the ancient, and also must relate to an utterly opposite way of being than we are able to conceive of from within the box of modern thinking. This is what makes writing about this difficult. It is not an attack on modern culture but it is a stark reality of what modern culture really means in its words, ideas, music, art.

If we see the simplicity and connect to nature which is innate in the ancient material, it becomes clear that although we have forgotten this language it speaks to a deep sense of "OurSelf", often in fact that which has no words or cognition. This is the reason why in this book I will be very careful to avoid using Western medical terms and expression where possible. On the rare occasions when I do, I will assume that there is an understanding of difference between the modern western idea, for example, of a separate organ called a "heart" and the meaning of this in energetic medicine which isn't just the physical organ of the heart but includes this and the "nature" or energy of this organ throughout the individual body and also the whole of universal nature as a resonant energetic expression of the beat of life. If one considers these items as expressions of a spectrum of energy, we are closer to the mark and closer to understanding medical Oneness.

medical oneness

chapter 4

The principle of Medical Oneness: rediscovering our instinctive universal language

In the next sections, we will discuss the philosophy of yinyang as a basis for energetically understanding the human and a foundation to our communication with each other. To begin, I will just look at what yinyang means in classical Taoist terms and how we can link this with ancient Greek and other ancient medical principles. I will then enter into the beginnings of energetic diagnostics, simply using yinyang. Please understand that this is the pure principle without specifics, it is a very broad angle and encompassing. In the next sections, I will consider how we can apply the principles to contextualize and understand the plethora of theories and tools on offer in the world of medicine and how the spectrum of medicine can be understood, with all its crossover applications of different expressions, contextualizing the medical tree from its specific branches.

Let us start with the background roots, the principles, the origin from which we can have a conversation, our common language, which is not embedded in a country or in a tradition, but in our very sense and instinct.

Principles of YinYang - the universal diagnostic language

Yinyang is not a purely Chinese idea. In fact, most symbols of ancient times provide an expression of seeming dual and opposing force coming together as one. Yinyang is really the most sought-after pictorial equation that modern quantum theory cannot yet fathom as it is still looking at specific notions not at everything at once. Yinyang is the understanding that all expansions or movements are balanced by accumulations or non-movements. The yang is the principle of heat and light, the yin of cold and darkness. The heat and light displaces the cool and dark, and the cool and dark occurs after the heat and light recede. They seem to follow one another in cycles and they seem to grow out of each other and balance each other. There is never a time where they are apart although it can seem like it: for example it can be daylight in Australia and dark in the UK at the same time but for the person in the UK it is dark. The key point is that yinyang is a way of describing all phenomena within the circle of Oneness. Nearly all creation ideologies from around the world generally express Oneness forming two-ness, and from there on, myriad creation. The idea of yinyang, therefore, is an example of an expression. The yinyang symbol itself is uniquely perfect due to its being circular in every aspect of its image and formation. This non-edge means there is no point at which there is an absolute. The yinyang symbol is absorbed easily into all ancient cultures and used as if a part of, or illustrative of, the main understanding at the heart of the expression. Therefore, when I explain using yinyang and terms of Chinese origin, we must understand that it is really an echo of the ancient world to which I am adhering, rather than proposing Taoist ideology as superior. As we will see, "Taoist ideology as superior" is an impossible notion, as Taoist expression is always about acknowledging non-duality. Below is the yinyang symbol. Notice, in particular, the black square backing the symbol, as this is how the symbol should always be presented:

The black backing the symbol and the circle itself, rather than the dual images within the circle, represent Oneness. Please note that the Oneness backs or envelops the foreground of the white yang movement. Notice, too, that the yin, or black aspect, is only understood and known by the yang's displacing movement. This is the entire important philosophy of ancient understanding in one expression - the foreground and the background. The background is always constant and always behind; it is the universal principle of Oneness, no-thing-ness, the Origin of yinyang, which is everything-ness. Hence yinyang is enveloped by the Original Oneness. What is very important is that we get an understanding of the differentiation of foreground and background.

Seeming separateness: the foreground

Here, in the foreground of life, meaning the world of the human who sees all things as apart, separate from him/herself, everything is duality. (Interestingly, "the devil" in the original Latin, means "the divider.") The point is that the total focusing of what is in the foreground of our lives, i.e. our direction outwards into the world of objects and things, and our seeking ourselves outwards in the world, leads us to look for our root in the foreground. This always ends up with a vicious circle, that which we call dis-ease or sufferance.

Please see in the diagram this represents the white only, not recognizing the black, or background, this is the yang only. As explained above when yang is warped and fails to be its normal expansive open expression of life, in humans it forms a contracted "self-image". This is dis-ease in itself, it is the idea and belief in a separate self not contextualized by the background yin. Contraction therefore is a very particular word which is really associated with dis-ease state. We can't really say yin is contractive as there is no intention behind yin or no force, it is accumulative, brings things together and is a backing density, but it cannot be said to be contractive. All contraction is a yang action whether the contraction of a muscle which is a natural event or in the case of speaking about dis-ease and health contraction always meaning dis-ease.

Oneness: the background (that which holds the foreground)

When the background is considered as primary (this is also the circle that holds the yinyang as one), then there is a totally different way of understanding. Firstly, "I" cannot be differentiated from "you"; we are one and the same. The foreground is not separate from anything, it is simply an expression of Oneness. This could be explained as a broad perspective versus a narrow perspective, and phrases like "not seeing the wood for the trees" are examples of this. Oneness is inclusive by nature. It is in fact this background knowing of Oneness which drives all aspects of our lives, even if we believe the world to contain separate people. This applies to everything from the obvious, like the sexes coming together to form unity, the various charitable and family -orientated ways of being, religious gatherings and so on. But it also applies where we would least expect it: to the murderer, the rapist, the criminal, the capitalist. In all cases, they feel that they are on their own, separate, so the attempt is always to bring the universe to Oneness however warped this may seem. They attempt to control a person, then a family, then a town, then the world, then the universe. Once everything is controlled, or killed for that matter, which is a form of control here, then it comes to Oneness; it has eventually found its root again. So in non-duality, there is no saint and no sinner, no higher and no lower; both are one and the same and there can never be a morally correct way. Anarchy in the original Greek means "without force, without direction"; this is key. The direction isn't coming from individualism but from a wholeness. In fact, anarchy is the expression of spontaneous natural order, the way of nature.

Natural medicine has this as its fundamental root and the background view allows us to accept everything, all forms of medical practice, like a sponge. It allows us to bring them all in, see them all as tools of the same Source and therefore suitable in the situations for which they are appropriate. Through our natural expression of being what we are as medical practitioners, we no longer need to adhere to the tool used in a treatment, but rather to the underlying principle that is at its heart. The tool we have in our hand therefore becomes an instrument of the instinct we are born with, and so drives us towards a particular expression of the Oneness. This is our truest and easily flowing authentic self, which cannot be contrived or forced into a box. This connects to the universe and allows for a return to a natural paradise, where nothing is forsaken in life or death. There is no dis-ease. This is an ideal, obviously. Yinyang is a mental tool. Firstly, it allows us to know the true nature of reality through constantly reminding us of the background, the Oneness that is the original. Secondly, from this perspective of stillness or objectively seeing how things are as they are, yin in relation to yang - the expression of a human body, a plant, a sunrise, anything at all can be seen as a balance of yinyang expressional forces in relation to each other. Yinyang is a way of mentally considering all things as relative opposite qualities. All things can be considered relatively if one takes a contextual perspective, the background that underpins the foreground. Whatever your perspective, yinyang functions, as it is the expression of all things.

Let's look more into the yinyang principle: Yinyang is the foundational block for observing and studying the universe. Yin is always displaced by yang. Yin is still. Yang is light. Yin is dark. Lightness displaces darkness, yet the darkness still exists. Yin corresponds to the archetypal female, and yang to the male, although this relates only to a basic stereotype.

Yin	Yang
Earth (also connected to void)	Heaven
Autumn and winter	Spring, summer
Sour and bitter flavours	Pungent, sweet and salty flavours
Female (archetype - fire)	Male (archetype-water)
Soft (but dense)	Hard (but energetic)
Slow to change	Fast to change
Dense	Diffused
Calm/ stillness	Change
Silence	Sound
Dark	Light
Accumulating	Expanding
Deep	Superficial
Inside	Outside
Cold	Heat
Receptive	Penetrating
Below	Above
Absorbing in	Radiating/giving off
Physical	Energetic
Body	Spirit

Just to clarify the point, in ancient Greek wisdom, the relative yinyang principle was characterized by Aristotle as heat-dry/cold-wet. Since Pythagorean times these form the basis of the five elemental phases of Greek medicine. In Ayurvedic understanding, the origination of life came from two aspects: Purusha and Prakruti. That which is formless and spaceless and timeless, a naked background awareness of no-thingness was called Purusha, which relates to void and yin, although it has male attribution, which makes it like water (see above). Prakruti is the counter-energy to Purusha, it is everything-ness, light and movement and form. It relates to yang but also to fire, which has female expression (see above). This forms the basis for the Indian 5 elements or phases, which form the "dosha" system of Ayurveda. The point is that whatever the mix of qualities and variation of the idea, the yinyang is at the heart of this expression. It forms the origin of the five phases and three doshas of Indian medicine.

The background is what this book is describing or pointing towards - Oneness, the origin. Yinyang is the manifestation of manifold natural formations that express themselves in the universe. Here we can visually depict the very singularity of expression from Oneness. All of the yang energy, or white in the above symbol, can collectively be called yang, or Heaven energy. The yin energy, or black aspect of the symbol (including the background), can be called yin, or Earth, but it also represents Void/the Origin. One can say that the original Void or Stillness was there before life on earth began. At the point of change or the "Big Bang" as it is called in modern science, first yang-Heaven and yin-Earth are formed, meaning the initial yang of creation i.e. heat, and then the more condensed energy of matter, or yin-Earth occur. So yang-Heaven is "given birth to" from the yin-like Void, then yin-Earth from within the yang-Heaven. Heaven and earth here do not have religious connotations at all but are merely representations of that which is rising and more energetic in relation to that which is more heavy and dense. In this book, I will go no further than yinyang. The energetic ABC is already within what we have looked at so far and as this is the foundation of the whole of our universal language and everything else on top of this is details which you yourself will easily be able to understand once the roots are clear, so I will focus here in our basic language only.

The five-phase is the next expression used by the ancient Chinese to describe further stage of expansion of Oneness; these themselves are segments of yinyang. However, they complicate matters and add more complex theory and explanation. In so far as we are talking about Oneness and separation, all we need to understand is yinyang as shown above, in order to find the root back to the source of medicine and also to know where we, as cells within this unified body, differ in expression, but cannot differ in source, at any point. The principle of yinyang can be applied to absolutely everything, from natural phenomena to politics, art and advertising, to forms of spiritual tradition, and issues of understanding cultural difference to the madness of racism, any seeming difference between anything on the surface of the world. Wittgenstein gives us the expression exactly: "The subject does not belong to the world: rather, it is a limit of the world." (Wittgenstein L., 1921), meaning that the subjective view is actually Oneness-viewing. There is only one subject, so to speak, and this subject is the background of the world. It *is* the world but is not *only* the world. It backs and underpins everything. Hence, one cannot talk about ideas of Oneness in terms of separation or talk about the background in terms of the foreground. Also one cannot talk about the foreground in terms of the background. The background is one with the foreground, so this has no terms. The foreground, however, wants to put things into terms, so it attempts to do so by categorizing its origin. This is like a snake eating its tail.

This is commonly the problem of attempting to express concepts of natural medicine in terms of Western medicine. This is impossible, as the modern ideology is the aspect that wants the idea of the background (which is like the head categorizing the feet it stands on!); the background already knows the foreground and has accepted it as an aspect of itself. The modern foreground,

41

however, wants to make it "integrated", wants to "fix" it by putting it into categorized and finite terms, but one cannot do this with that which is infinite. This is the problem. Einstein expressed this eloquently when he said, "No problem can be solved from the same level of consciousness that created it", meaning problems of mind-identity cannot be solved or understood from that level. It has to be solved from a place where the mind is contextualized, thinking outside of the box, so to speak. However, with this issue, we are speaking about that which is beyond even the thought process.

From these basic principles, we can move on to consider how they can be used in diagnostics of the human body, and in this consideration make a foundation principle for diagnosis that is not a matter of opinion, but is viewed from a point of objectivity.

Chapter 5

The practitioner, diagnostic universality, and unity with the patient

Now we come to the practitioners themselves. What is a practitioner? Why is one person a patient and one a practitioner? Who makes the choice? The key here is eloquently described in a Chinese proverb of unknown authorship: "A bird doesn't sing because it has the answer, it sings because there is a song." We don't choose. Free will implies a separate free will and this cannot be true. Being authentically ourselves is about listening and not resisting what it is that we are. In doing so, we come to know what we can innately do well and what we naturally find difficult, not because of some idea, a moral sense of duty or a detached concept, but because it is truly the full expression of what we are. This is merely a way of saying that one can only be what one is, no matter how hard one tries to be anything else. This of course is not suggesting that change is not possible, but that change means allowing nature to live through us and drive the process, of change, not "self"-directed change. Also, when I say "what one is," I mean the expression behind one's

43

idea of being a separate person in a world of separate people. I'm talking about the very Sense and True-Self - One with all things - that knows that he or she is a better violin player than a double bass player, or more happy with the drums than the saxophone. It's about the voice, your natural voice, one's natural note or vibrating resonance. It's in the song you sing, not the answer you are trying to arrive at; it's in the journey and the way you move, not the end result. This book attempts to connect to those who are spontaneously and naturally interested in medicine. Those who can give a "good reason" for doing it may not actually feel a call to be doing it; it may be a mask or disguise for another expression as yet unknown, or known and not acknowledged as "right " or "practical" or "morally correct".

There is no real reason for doing medicine at all. This is commonly called "selfish" in modern terms but actually being what one is, is the least selfish thing one can do. It is letting go of the idea that one has a choice in the matter, a self-less expression in fact. This leads to great effects with patients as there is a peace rather than a frustration with which one interacts. However, very often it is damaged by the ideology of a "system" of medicine and a hierarchical training, which clamps down on a natural intuitive sense and starts to block inwards, resulting in what we see in modern medicine today - healers who have no expression for their healing. This is a great shame, the way of *all* ancient medicines is to use what is at hand and to remember the innate senses.

The practitioner/patient relationship

The practitioner who was able to see things as they are, rooted in the background of life, was known as the shaman, able to transcend the world of the mundane through the very acceptance of it, without any additions. To her/ his community she/ he was a vital resource and a re-connection to nature whenever the mind-identified state crept in and processes of dis-ease and lack of awareness of the environment took hold. The point is that, ideally, the doctor is naturally being, in the moment and one with the patient, sensing everything without judgment; this allows an impression of what *is* to be clear. When a practitioner is this, it seems miraculous to the people caught within analysis of her/ him, because it is as if she/ he is understanding something that is unfathomable. All she/ he is doing is looking to see the background, the context of the problem, and thereby seeing the general pattern as well as the specific symptoms in that pattern. She/ he doesn't focus on the symptoms but can see the root of the dis-ease, and so in focusing on this - which may be completely different what one expects the doctor to do - she/ he points to where the patient naturally wants to go, and as such seems to "cure" illness. The doctor did nothing except what was appropriate for engendering the best natural order, so can we even say it was she/ he who was involved in the outcome? Not really. This is the ideal of the practitioner, a force of nature, the resonance and expression of natural Oneness. This is what the healer is, even if he or she thinks that they are in command, that it's their energy doing it all. It doesn't matter what the theory is, nature will provide through them, no matterwhat resistance there is, although if there is resistance healing is probably not the right route of expression for them at that time.

From this perspective, how does the patient fit into all this? The practitioner ideally acknowledges the patient as himself/herself, sensing the natural instinct that the patient has, and then pointing towards this in some form, helping the patient to acknowledge that this instinct is the way back to health. For example, the practitioner helps the patient acknowledge the natural instincts to sleep when tired, eat when hungry, go to defecate and urinate when it is time, and to follow the natural cycles of day and season. The doctor helps the patient to instinctively know what food is right and how much to eat, to know when to move and to be active and when to be still and rest. These are some of the possible directions that the practitioner can draw the patient's attention to, so that a natural order might be free-flowing and the person might "automatically know" what to do and how to be, without a "reason why" or any input from a practitioner. The practitioner makes himself redundant as soon as possible, totally appropriate to the conditions. This therefore is less about the practitioner, although it is amazing how many modern practitioners and teachers of ancient medicine really make it all about them and yet announce otherwise. It is very clear when true medicine is occurring, as the patient will come to the conclusion themselves that they have found health, and then need for the practitioner becomes no more. Ideally there is no requirement on the part of the practitioner to gain acknowledgment or recognition as it is understood that what is "mine" is "yours" and Oneness means ownership, and dogmatic conventions are debunked. If not, it's all a façade for a kind of power-play. This also occurs between teacher-student relationships, although it is rare to find a teacher who has this kind of connection in the modern day, and often the student's learning becomes about uncovering what one can and looking towards nature as the teacher, not towards individualists with a corrupted idea of "lineage".

The "ideal" is simply natural Oneness, unity with that which is running the show anyway, acknowledgment of this, following rather than leading, allowing the mind-identity process to go into retirement, letting the body be taken over by that which is truly the "holy spirit" of natural sense. This, in Chinese, is called Qi; in Japan, *Ki*; in India, Prana; in ancient Greek, *Aether*; in Bon of Tibet, it is space; to the North American Indians, it is Spirit.

The point is that this fundamental Oneness that condenses into yin and the physical, or expands in yang and the immaterial, is the fundamental heat and cold of the universe and has no judgment - it is One. Whether or not modern physics has succeeded in getting close to this idea with "field" theory and the like, the true nature of this was known many thousands of years ago and is still known in what is a fuller expression, in terms of the animals and plants around us. If there are teachers, these are they.

Diagnostics

Having understood the true nature of a patient and practitioner and their Oneness, it is now relevant that we speak of diagnostics and how they are the interface that allows for the natural connection to be recognized in the modern world of seeming individuals. Integrative medicine seems to look towards fixing a problem or creating an "umbrella" to cover a many broken parts. Rather than this, if there could be a way for truly understanding a patient very, very simply, one that could be agreed upon by all practitioners at all times, this would be a foundation to herald medical Oneness, a true union of medicine beyond interpretation but known from sensitivity and sense.

Diagnostics involves the patient and interaction with them. We are no longer interested at this point in treating anything, just in seeing what *is*. Part of what *is*, are the symptoms. They provide some information, but we need to make an assessment not only of the symptoms but also of the whole person, in the context of their life. This means we need to look broadly. Oriental diagnosis, like that of all the ancient methods, involves the practitioner's senses picking up on the patient's issues. These senses are categorized as follows:

- Listening: This means listening to the patient's voice and the sound of it, not the words but the quality of the voice. Is it loud? Is it soft? Is it high? Is it low in pitch? What is it like?

- Smelling: The odour of the patient is detectable even through perfumes and other scents that attempt to hide it. If there is a smell or an absence of smell, this indicates something.

- Looking: The visual diagnostic is not about looking specifically at a part of the body but looking at that part in context with the rest. What looks out of place - too red, too pale, too black or blue? It is about what hits you as being odd in relation to what is constitutionally presented in the patient's body, or gives an impression of something jutting out. It may be obvious and bright or very lacking and dull.

- Touching: Palpatory diagnosis is the feeling of the pulses of the body, the touching of the skin and the general sensing of the musculature and areas of tightness and tension in theabdomen, the back, the limbs, and the trunk. The process of touching is in itself a healing, but it is also diagnostic, helping to find areas of tension and stagnation and areas of looseness and weakness.

- Questioning: Asking questions is the last approach, because it is used only to confirm the other diagnostics that are felt without words. The use of language and mind and cognition is something that is secondary because it is often inaccurate and distorted. The mind-identification - that is, the disease at the root - is speaking, and as such it can skew the information. Questioning can, however, help to decipher some things and can be useful when informed by the other four methods of diagnosis.

These five diagnostic procedures (leaving out taste for obvious reasons! and also due to the fact that it is considered to be part of the smelling diagnosis) use all the facilities the practitioner has. All are informed by a "sixth sense," so to speak, which is an innate knowing of the patient as one with the practitioner. This informs everything and is the basis for everything. Again, even in diagnostics, we must not get caught up in the process of obtaining information, but remain anchored in the background. So what do these diagnostics tell us? What can we assess from them? Let us look at the following list of yinyang expressions most used in relation to body diagnostics:

Yin Yang expressions most used in relation to body diagnostics

Yin Energy	Yang Energy
Cold	Hot
Below	Above
Accumulating	Expanding
Deficiency of heating energy (yang)	Deficiency of cooling energy(yin)
Soft and empty	Hard and full-tight
Tired	Awake
Interior related	Exterior related
Chronic	Acute
Pale/blue/white	Red/green/yellow
Sallow	Bright
No odour	Strong odour
Slow	Fast
Deep	Superficial
Quiet	Loud
Little to say	A lot to say
Grief, fear-terror, muddled-unclear	Anger, excitability, anxiety
Low consumption	High consumption
Inward looking	Outward looking
Sensitive	Insensitive
Victim, past focused	Aggressor, past projected into future focused
Seems depressed but is actually tired	Depression, mania, anger locked internally
Will tend to be either exhausted and quiet or exhibit some frustration at not being able to express; no energy to do so	Wants things their way, tends to be stuck, tight and rigid, or over-exited and over-pushy/irritated

These above ideas give a picture of yinyang that we can use clinically. When assessing a patient, we need to understand them in terms of being either yin-deficient or yang-deficient. The deficient aspect is always the root of the problem. What is weak is always what is "sought" by the patient, whether they know it or not; it is the aspect of them that they need and can't find. They move towards finding the thing they need, but often in ways that are distorted from their natural instinct. The practitioner points the patient back to instinct, back to natural health. The above are observations one would obtain in the course of diagnosis. The practitioner would then find one of the two following patterns: the yang-deficient pattern (yin energy is stronger here), or the yin-deficient pattern (yang energy is stronger here). For the yang-deficient pattern, when I say yin energy is stronger, I mean that the person is cooler. For humans, this means closer to death, if we think of life being like fire. Hence, humans overall are closer to fire than ice, so death is colder rather than hotter than our body temperature in life. Therefore, yang deficiency is relative to the exterior (i.e. cold relative to the climate), whereas yin deficiency is relative to the inside (i.e. hot relative to what they would be in a balanced state). When I say "balanced state," I mean for that person's constitution, *not* what is right for a person of a particular age on a chart or on a pre-created scale, but where that person is right now. This is the only real scale available. Is it right - right now - or not?

Yin deficiency pattern

The patient comes in. He (tends to be more male pattern) will have a red complexion and speak in a loud voice. He will find it hard to sit still in the chair, will be open, and will express himself easily. He won't be shy, and may be anxious or tense, but he tells you about it. It probably involves working too much, a very stressful job, and doing more than he can do. He has goals and he has a large social network. He will have, on palpation, a full pulse with some power in it that you can easily feel at the surface of the skin. His abdominal muscles and the muscles over his body will be slightly taut and tight. He may complain of back tension, usually in the upper back and the neck/shoulder region. He is most likely to come to you for an acute injury or tension in the upper body or an upper-body-related symptom. It is more likely that he is constipated and dehydrated because of the heat in his body. In this case the patient has a strongly contracted and usually heavily ego-dominated mind-identity which directs him towards addictive behaviour encouraging more of the same - it is a cycle that moves towards a limit point or breaking point mental-emotionally.

Yang deficiency pattern

The second pattern is yang deficiency. This person is cold and she (more stereotypically female) will be tired generally. She is pale and lethargic and more still than moving. She will have a weaker voice. She may have a lot to say, but it will make her tired to express it all, so she would prefer to just lie down. She will look sallow, overworked, and fatigued. She may be sad, grief-stricken, fearful, phobic, muddled, or confused. She will like the warm and hate the cold. She will generally not have an appetite, or at least it will be reduced. Everything will be pale and weak-looking. The issue will tend to be a chronic case and not an acute problem, often related to low energy and problems resulting from this. In this case the patient has a weaker but active mind-identity contraction which is often of the egoic state of the "victim". This too can seem unchangeable. It moves the patient into self-protective states of a want to be cared for, which is partially appropriate but which forms a "weak" self-image that is hard to change. It generally is chronic and moves towards a gradual letting-go process rather than a breaking point disaster.

The two pictures give a very different outlook, expressing two very different pictures of dis-ease. Aetiologically, the yin-deficient person will tend to have more internally-based issues from addiction to a particular way of being, including eating or doing something that is damaging his body. The yang-deficient type will have dis-ease due also to internal reasons, for example, believing in a diet that is "good" for her, when in fact it is the opposite in effect, and being addicted to doing this too. Yang deficiency pattern also has an exterior factor of climate and environment that could be making her problem worse (i.e. cooling her down beyond her ability to keep warm). The yin-deficient pattern is not affected by the exterior so much. If it is too hot, he sweats, if too cool, he enjoys it because he is too warm. He is, in fact, in a healthier state than she is because he has warming energy which balances itself out. She needs more heat and therefore is always in need of more energy.

Of course, clinically these two patterns do not present themselves so clearly, and there will be a mix of male and female with both of them. However, the practitioner needs to distinguish, using his or her senses, whether the patient *overall* is more hot or more cold. If more of the signs and symptoms point to heat, then the main symptoms the patient has will be associated with inflammation and tension and heat. If most of the signs and symptoms point to cold (even though some may be heat-related), then cold will be the source of her symptom picture. The confusing two patterns in Chinese are known as true cold with false heat, meaning the pattern is cold but some of the symptoms relate to heat, and true heat with false cold, which is the opposite. Again, the key is to see the overall picture, not the symptoms only. This then becomes the basis for whatever form or healing one uses to effect change. Any healing, no matter what kind, can affect the patient in a way that improves this pattern. If the diagnosis is incorrect and the incorrect treatment approach is used, it can cause a worsening of the problem. Generally most approaches take the allopathic point of view which is the balance of opposites to create stability within the body. Allopathy means that if she is too cool, heat her up; if he is too hot, cool him down. It's this simple. Allopathy, in this true sense of the word, treats the root, which is always a deficiency within the system.

Supplementary to this are other methodologies, like homeopathy and cathartic treatment processes which treat like with like, so for example, if the patient is too hot one heats them a little more, to ideally push the patient's mechanism to re-balance itself; this however is rarely used to treat the deficient root of the pattern. Cathartic methods are used exclusively on the patients who are yin-deficient and too hot in primal medicine. The ideology, if one sees it in completeness, is always to bring about the reduction of the symptoms, but from instinctive foundation always to do this from the root, hence allopathic methodology is the foundation and homeopathic-cathartic methods are supplementary to this, or are used for acute and over-heated problems. All healing methods are contained within this expression of heat and cold, whether it is light therapy, crystals, acupuncture, herbal medicine, Reiki, or any other methodology. It is all about bringing the right connection of energetic quality to the body in order to wake up its own instinctual resonance; the tool is not the issue, it's the theory through which one looks at it.

This all sounds very body-orientated, without consideration of the personality or way-of-being, in the ancient understanding called the "spirit" expression of the person. Mind originally was an extension of the function of "spirit" but it has now taken over to be a self-image creating illusion in dis-ease state. Hence the focus of natural medicine is always on body-spirit, mind is secondary and is calmed when body-spirit is allowed to be as it is. Body can be considered yin and spirit yang (mind is very yang!) so in fact all we are talking about is the yinyang of the human. Some people are naturally cooler and some naturally hotter in the expression of their personality. This, too, is an important assessment and must be considered. However, a person who has dis-ease will never be affected only in the body or the spirit, they are totally unified. Hence, dis-ease within the heat-cold spectrum tells of dis-ease within the spirit; it shows, in fact, that the body-spirit is directing its energy, not towards "as it is" but more towards "as they wish things to be" or "as it was." Be they "future" anxiety-driven projections from the past, or past often depression-based reflections, these are always the places that the expression of the spirit gets caught. In sensing the personality-spirit of the person, one can also know that they may have a weak body but have a fiery personality, or they may have a powerful body but have a soft and gentle personality. It is often the case that the body and spirit qualities are opposite and don't seem to match, but matching is not what medicine is about. Acceptance as a whole is what medicine is about, so the process of bringing about cooling or heating to the body in whatever form, including psychotherapeutics, can have a more warming or cooling effect. This will bring about relaxation, whatever the balance of body-spirit qualities are.

This is not a belief system, it is common-observational. The same etiology of dis-ease causes a very different process for two people of different personalities and very similar body structures, or symptoms present differently with similar personality but different body structures. Practitioners must always hold the background view. Their role is to allow what "is" to be, and to indicate the movement towards the instinct of nature through the patient's needs. This approach is easy, direct, and offers no resistance. Patients that resist the process are not ready. Practitioners who force the process are also not ready. Nature is always in command, so appropriateness to *what is*, is the only real process here. Hence, as far as signs and symptoms go, the healing of these can be accessed through the body and/or spirit, depending on the medicine you choose. Either way, the healer will need to acknowledge the facts of *what is*. No matter how subtle or obvious the healing method is, the direction of it must acknowledge the universally understood symptoms of heat and cold, or yinyang. Once a pattern is understood as an overall generalized idea, then the chosen medicine can be applied appropriately. The practitioner can refer the patient to other practitioners, depending on whether the majority of signs and symptoms manifest around the subtle or more physical energetics.

Of course there will be constant crossover in the effects of what different individual practitioners can affect in healing situations. The point is to acknowledge the facts before this is investigated. The constitution of the person before dis-ease is what we need to see, it is behind the mask of what has occurred. The question is, does this person seem healthy and whole, or are they moving away from health and wholeness; and secondly, how/why are they doing this? The answers are fundamentally simple at root and in all cases always have a root-anxiety of a sense of separation/contraction that needs to be let go, then healing just happens.

Deficiency

The root of dis-ease is always deficiency. This is a key point and we must be clear about why. Deficiency means "relative lack of" and so it manifests as a weakness in the system. Whether it is a bridge or a human, the part where there is a weakness will be the part that causes the main problem which leads to collapse. It is the area of the system where energy has been drawn away from, due to the dis-ease state and contraction of suffering/ mind-identity. The idea of treatment is always to allow the weakness to be acknowledged and return to being part of the whole, not numbed or without aliveness. When a weakness is strengthened, all functions of the bridge or human or building, or any structure at all, become more prolific, more expanded, and more useful. Weakness is sometimes invisible because it is a lack of something, not a strength of something. Strengths tend to be seen, front and present, while the back of the issue tends to be hidden, invisible and not present. As practitioners, we have to be aware of this as the main issue - symptoms present themselves due to an overall lack, and an overall lack will create an overall strength in the opposite of what the patient needs, i.e. more heat or more cold. In every case, if the weakness can be responded to with the appropriate treatment, then the body-spirit maintains its integrity. If not, at the very end, the body-spirit changes form. This is commonly called death, a total resolution of the contraction of mind-identity.

Note therefore that dis-ease is a process of the body whereby it changes form and moves towards death, which is a sense is an ultimate cure or resolution of the problem, whereas curing in healing is the process of healing the deficient root and moves towards life, but is a letting-go within life of the resistance/ contraction. So this process in fact is also a death, but within life. Both situations are an acknowledgement of the yin, the background, the body-spirit rather than the mind-identity. Neither situation is good or bad. Although we call it "deficiency" this is just in terms of life; we could also call it strengthening of death! In both yin or yang deficiency the root of the problem is always the contracted state of the mind, but the way to resolve this is impossible through the contraction itself, rather through the area of weakness and a reconnection therefore to wholeness and openness. Suffering/contraction is always the root, yinyang is the diagnostics of the "damage" done by this contraction and therefore the method one takes energetically to resolve the contraction indirectly though the allopathic natural balancing of energy. If we look at this contraction or suffering overall we can say that it is a yang-phenomenon and that the background yin is missing from view. This is very much what we see in the world as a whole - the yang-dominated society based in hierarchy, power, control, dominance over other and arrogant narrowness. This is quite contrary to Christ's recognition of the yin when he explains: "blessed are the meek for they shall inherit the earth", meaning that it is those who can actually see the nature of the earth and have breadth of vision that inherit, and in fact are part of its innate wisdom. Fundamentally in relation to the contraction of yang that is mind-identity, or the root of dis-ease, it is the yin which is the basic fundamental principle of cure in medicine. In yang deficiency this contraction occurs with cold body-spirit symptoms, in yin deficiency the contraction has more power and occurs with an overheated body-spirit. It is always that the words are inadequate and the instinct clear when it comes to understanding root medicine.

Treatment principle

Although the therapeutic method itself can vary, based on our diagnosis of either yin deficiency or yang deficiency, the following principles associated with treatment will always apply. This can help us refine the tool we are using and adjust to what we find with the patient's present condition.

Yang-deficient treatment principles

Warm the body; don't cool the body. Don't allow the person to be in a draught. Don't allow the person to get so hot that they sweat and cool off. It is always better to warm from the inside out rather than from the surfaces inwards. If your method is associated only with the surfaces, then attempt to cover and treat the very surfaces of the body. Deep tissue massage is not appropriate. Manipulation and aggressive procedures are not appropriate either. Generally, unless it is an absolute life or death situation, surgery is *not* appropriate. Foods that are raw and cooling and hard to digest are not appropriate; foods need to be warm and easy to digest. The salty, sweet, and pungent tastes are appropriate, with only a very limited amount of sour and bitter-flavoured foods and herbs. Don't speak too much to the patient. Rather, allow them to sleep during the treatment, if possible. When you must speak, do so with a soft voice, making everything slow and soothing. Don't use strong pressure massage, and don't allow the patient to have long, hot baths. They may have short, hot baths or short showers. The patient should do limited exercise, just enough for circulation and movement, until the patient feels warm all over, yet not to the point of sweating as this lets out heat.

Yin-deficient treatment principles

Cool the body down, and calm the patient down. Don't do a lot of frantic movement around the head and neck. If you need to work there, do so deeply and slowly. You can do more movement down the body and in the feet, for there quick movements can be made without a problem. It is best to cool the patient down from the outside inwards, making exterior treatment methods the most appropriate. If you have only interior methods of treatment, use food and herbs that cool the body down; these will reduce the content of saltiness, sweetness, and spiciness and increase sourness and bitterness. Vegetarian foods are best, particularly foods that are white and green in colour, rather than red and orange. Longer, hot baths are appropriate here, as are sweating and exercise. The primary, most important methodology needs to include releasing heat from the body via the pores of the skin. Enemas, colonics, and deep massage are all appropriate. Any treatment of the skin that allows the blood circulation to come to the surface and open the pores is also appropriate. All cathartic methods of treatment are appropriate. Surgery should be done only when necessary but is more appropriate for this condition and will generally be beneficial. Cleansing dietary programs are all appropriate here.

The above overviews give us general principles to work with. Again, nothing is absolute here, there is always a balance of yinyang to determine, when making a diagnosis. However, these two broad categories define all of the people we will see as patients, and the lists of relative symptom patterns are endless. As such, it is a foundational base to work from and use as a universal language helping us to contextualize the tools we have so that mono-treatment doesn't occur but rather, adaptive, natural, responsive, and sensitive connection - appropriate healing for the patient which is directly expressive of the healer. Up until this point, we haven't really spoken about therapeutics. So far, we are just assessing what is going on with the patient, looking at the signs and symptoms in a very broad way, the pure evidence of what is happening now at every level. We are looking at everything from the expression of past issues that are felt emotionally, to the physical signs and symptoms of the body, from the existential struggles of the heart to the broken limb. If we wanted to, we could get lost in the whole story, the intricacies and nuances of the difficulties the patient is having within their life. Instead, the practitioner stays back and yet is one with the patient. They are in the background and grounded, so that they can be an anchor to the patient's expression, not taken along by the flow of the dis-ease, not affected but not detached, intimate yet impersonal.

This gives a platform to consider one's way/tool, not the label of theoretical position you take, and the way/tool of all the practitioners one knows contextually, in order to determine what is suitable for this patient at this time. What is appropriate amongst the tools at universal disposal and extending this further, who would be best to see this patient? This is not about seeing what you want another practitioner to be in relation to you, and so referring when you feel that the label-training of your colleague is "right" for them, but actually more like understanding who your colleague is and realizing that this might be best for the patient, they are the right tool of interaction, not the right "label" like "osteopath" or "nutritionist", which is merely linking to a theoretical ideal, which as we will see, is usually limited. It's not an energetic connection to each other, which is more basic, but more like a kinship, a realization or recognition of what the other person is. The diagnostic process is objective. The healing, too, comes from objectivity, but it also has an individual - the practitioner - at the end of it, who is also a tool of Oneness, and his/ her tool or treatment is an extension of their hand. The question is: does this patient match this practitioner for the issue at hand? Is he warm enough for her? Is she cool enough for him? Does it work like a marriage of expression? This is what Medical Oneness could be, if we are all singing from the same song-sheet, so to speak. Even though each of our voices is distinct, they are simply different vocal chords expressing the same tune.

The point is that the theoretical model is the basis from which people can restrict the way the instrument of healing (the practitioner and his/her equipment), could be used. In this book we are not really interested in the tools of the trade but the basic fundamental ideas behind the focus of the tools' use and the repercussion of this. People adhere to ideas and theories, not really to tools. Hence it is to the theoretical models labelled and classed as specific genre that cause separation, not the actual tools or techniques themselves. What this means is that potentially all therapists are healing, but the limitation

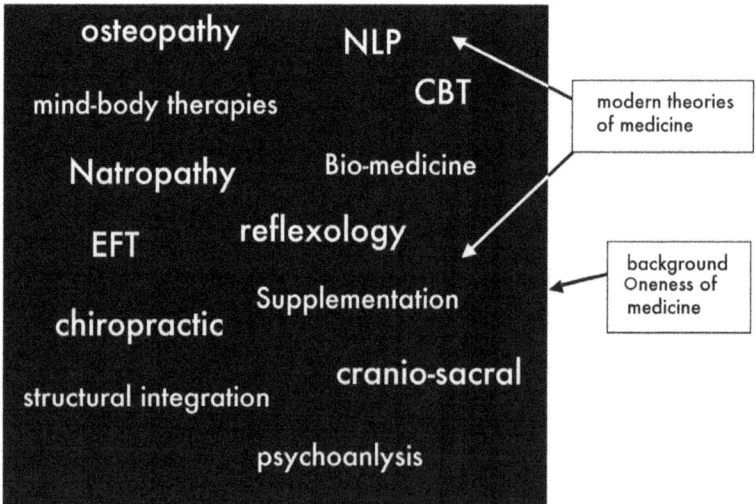

to their healing takes place in how they are thinking about their practice and their identification with theory, especially of the modern type of mind to body-spirit idea which is a very new occurrence and part of the dis-eased mind of separation rather than the curative process which is body-spirit instinct.

Intuitive or common-sense level connection is the key to diagnosis. In the moment that someone looks like they are getting a cold, you might say, "You look tired. Why don't you lie down?" That's diagnosis and healing in one. Simply responding to normal, everyday experiences is the key to instinctual health. It allows us to know ourselves and go with the flow instead of pushing against it. The physician has to be in the network of healing themselves, therefore, in order to recognize dis-ease in another person, otherwise, they will always miss it because they are caught up in theory, mind-identification, and their own illness. In the next chapter, we will look at the plethora of medical labels, beginning with a number of the natural medicines on offer. We will consider the big picture of medicine as a tree with roots and branches, and see how this can be used to understand the future of medicine, including what is relevant, what the tools are and how the theories that govern them do have an ancient root which is often ignored and so limiting the perspective of the practitioner.

3. Modern
(leaves) fragmented medicine without root:
naturopathy, chiropractic medicine, osteopathy, supplement theory, colonic irrigation
bio-resonance, allergy testing, supplementation,nutrition therapy, modern western
biomedicine. etc.
Head-downwards view.

**2. 'New Age' Medicine
 (branches)**
Name changing gradually
losing touch with the root.
Traditional Chinese medicine
(TCM), numerous styles of
acupuncture, shiatsu,
alexander technique,
homeopathy, reiki,
kinesiology, modern
astrology
(not ancient astrology),
crystal healing, tarot,
re-connective therapy,
sotai, cranio-sacral osteopathy,
hypnosis, reflexology etc.

1. Ancient

(root) medicinal culture (from around 500 BC), mainly Chinese,
Indian, and Greek, as well as Shamanic healers from around the world
with no method of practice but still appropriate. Techniques of these
medicines are acupuncture, herbal medicines, massage, surgery, and all
forms of healing that have been thought of by the above cultures and are
now called something different. Roots/ feet upwards

Chapter 6

The theories of healing and treatment: from ancient to modern

The theories of medicine associated with the "leaves" at the top of the tree are most accepted by Western medicine. As a result, the majority of people perceive them as the most "important" port of call after the doctor. In fact, referrals are often made to the top of the tree, but seldom to the whole-tree-perspective and roots. The second rung of the branches view are generally the forms of medicine that have a view which is beginning to expand outwards but which are now considered by the "leaf view" as lesser and lower in effect and importance. Those we can call "New Age" rather than modern, their practitioners are people who are interested in energy, rather than in the modern ideology of mechanism and physicality, but they are at a bridging point in their understanding and often need a methodology in western terms in order to be understood. Classical ancient medicine makes up the roots and the background, coming from Oneness - notice that the roots are part of the earth, and this is the "context" as well as the life force of the tree, they are the original idea that everything else is founded on. One of these ancient ways is Classical Chinese Medicine, (as distinct from its modern-day equivalent, now available all over the world in the form of "Traditional Chinese Medicine" (TCM), which is a fragmented version of the original understanding); these ancient medicines form the basis for everything else, including surgical techniques, which are not purely part of the leaf-view medicine by any means. Surgery is a tool not a theory. The technology of the knife may have changed, but the cut is still the same.

As we work from background view/roots to branch view and leaf view, rather than a story of "advancing" medicine what we find is that modern medicine is focused on the foreground, on the upper leaves, on the higher branches of the tree, very much associated with the head; whereas the ancient roots go back to the origin, and as such have valuable information that we have lost in the modern day. With this ever-fragmenting mental picture, we lose the trees and focus on the wood. Modern medicine in its theoretical position is blind to some areas, they are unable to see, except for the leaves over which they have control. Their practitioners are specialists, their tools are therefore specialized and restricting, following the theoretical base to their "specialization", unable to handle the underlying generality. They therefore force patients into categories of their own design and attempt to make the patients fit the tool. This doesn't work - nature doesn't form around ideas based on separation, except to further the nature of separation! Nature's design in fact, is the only true way, as Charles Darwin pointed out, earthworms have been ploughing and aerating the soil for millions of years before the invention of the plough and mono-culture farming. It is only now, with the realization of a crisis in oil production peaking, that attention is being given to the ancient way, which is following natural ways expressed by the ancient Taoist practice of Feng Shui and also in the modern expression of this in the permaculture movement. Any attempt to manipulate it from a restricted viewpoint will always be an act of force, and so inevitably will have the opposite reaction in the bigger picture. Yin always balances yang within the universe, as they are always tied to each other. It is not possible to see one without reference and reverence to the other. Everything is a phase, which will revert to the other, once that one is over, so there is always a balance occurring.

Please consider that there is a distinct difference between "healing" and "treatment." Healing might be thought of as a full picture of medicine and as such treats the context of the whole patient. A treatment might be considered as a healing process, restricted by a world-view or cultural modernism that blocks or impedes the healing process so it is inefficient and limited in its effect. This may be overridden by the practitioner's own intuitive sense but the theory in and of itself, if it starts with restriction, is a larger hurdle for the innate sense of the practitioner to overcome than a complete universal background or root understanding backing up the healing process; so intuitive sense matches theoretical expression, instinct informs theory and theory is a map to instinct which works for all cases without requiring a belief system. This is a yinyang model.

Let us look at each of these therapies individually. Each medicine will be considered from the perspective of the background whole, including how its view is contextualized by the whole and what its theoretical pitfalls are.

1. Ancient medical therapeutics
classical Chinese medicine healing therapies

The theory of Chinese medicine has been discussed above and is an example of a universal perspective so this is a good place to start. I will use the word "classical" associated with root-medicine meaning from the thread of the original medicine, but usually referring to a literary writing based in instinctual practice. (In China this would be Taoist medicine, rooted in prehistoric shamanism originally). Not all ancient cultures have a written tradition.

In Classical Chinese Medicine there are numerous branches which we can categorise into two main expressions: one is of the purely energetic tools, while the others seem more physical in approach. The energetic tools include the art of divination, counselling based on the understanding of cosmological signs and their relation to human personality or spiritual expression, hypnotics and meditation exercises. It also includes forms of training meant to bring the body to natural movement, such as Tai Chi, Qi Gong, (Qi Gong being a hands-off and also hands-on healing method), and Feng Shui (one's kinship with one's environment, as far as objects and other people and relationships go). The more physical healing therapies are more commonly known - they include acupuncture, herbal medicine, meridian-based or energetic-focused massage (massage of the whole body), micro blood-letting, moxibustion (heat therapy using mugwort burnt close to or on the skin surface), cupping, surgery, enemas, and cathartic purging.

All of these methodologies, and more, create the spectrum of the tools of Classical Chinese Medicine which is unrestricted in its expression, and which is both interior and physical and exterior and energetic. Even here there is a yinyang balance. This spectrum of medicine is the broadest, most variable range of tools - more so than any of the other ancient medical forms we have knowledge of, possibly because of the varied climate and arena of China itself. All tools are applied using the background principles already spoken of in this book, but the deepest root of the yinyang principle is the heart of this medicine. If this general principle is known, then it means unity in understanding, no matter what refinement is added. The basics are the foundation, without them the house will fall. The roots of medicine include the background and "soil", it is hidden below the surface, invisible but perpetual. Through whatever season, the roots remain alive and vibrant, even when the leaves have come off the tree. This indicates that classical medicine incorporates the whole tree. A practitioner is a specialization of this whole tree. They have a part to play and they will usually train in an expression of the medicine which suits them best, considering who they are. However, this is always in the context of the roots, hence the individual is not an individual but a part of the whole. Therefore, whatever the tool is, as long as the roots are connected to the leaves, they stay alive and well; the expression stays free from subjectivity and appropriate for the patient at a particular time. Referrals are made to other practitioners when necessary, with ease, like parts of the same hand.

Shamanism/spiritual healing/hands-on or hands-off healing

Shamanism is the root of all medicines. All over the world, around 500 BC, shamanism was beginning to lose its foothold, becoming distorted by people who considered shamanism as a power over others. This began to break down shamanism as root medicine. As a result, a new medicine emerged, less tainted with the past ideology of belief and more about seeing what there was, which of course harked back to the very foundations of shamanism itself in natural instinct. This new energy medicine became a pure-science of observation and common-sense (which will be discussed later), but which is a far cry from modern ideas of medicine. This occurred in almost all societies of the world at approximately 500 BC - as if human consciousness had reached a point of losing faith in dogmatic ideas and renewing its bonds with nature. Taoism, Hinduism, and the age of Hippocrates were the results in the ancient world. The difficulty has always been to separate the shamanic practitioner from the charlatan. Only the shamanic practitioner is indeed deeply sensing and considering his or her patient objectively. This problem is not something we can be free of, from inside or outside modern biomedicine, as it is also a problem in the New Age medicines and even in the root medicines themselves. In the end, a doctor who understands life will always draw patients, and one who cannot will inevitably fall by the wayside and do something else more suited to him/her.

The people involved in this kind of work are very often not able to explain why they can do healing. They cannot teach it (although they may profess to) but instead can just hope to instigate or initiate an awareness in another person to feel it themselves; they cannot learn it, it is seen by others as a miraculous gift. However, some notable practitioners, such as Joao Teixeira de Faria (known as "John of God"), Eric Pearl and Harry Edwards and numerous, less famous others, are considered healers and are associated with medicinal marvels and impossible cures. These practitioners generally have their own explanations about how they got the gift of healing, but they are unique individuals, and as such don't usually have a practicable method that can be taught. This is because during such healings the thought process and ideology is easily given up and they tend to be highly unrestricted people in healing, natural healers, who simply do what they do, usually without much need to question it. The theory isn't the healer and this is clear in these cases so the tool of healing is unrestricted. This is very much the foundation of medicine, but the theories that these healers then may speak of is not necessarily the whole picture of what they do, as modern language and belief systems held outside the healing process infiltrate the conversation. This takes nothing away from the actual healing, they are simply purely intuitive and usually utterly appropriate as practitioners.

The Shamans of various cultures today, in Mongolia, Africa, North and South America, Australia and elsewhere, especially when found in tribal societies, are able to instigate healing processes as a handed-down tradition, unwritten, but as a deeply felt and sensed expression. These cultures have a deep understanding of universality of natural laws, whether it be the North American Indians, the Shaman of Mongolia or the Aboriginal and Maori Medicine people. The formulation of healing into a learnt process with a written tradition and mentally-orientated access was rarely found. More common is the intuitive sense of being a healer or being chosen to be one by those who have sensitivity. Ancient medicine in all its forms probably originated from thousands of years of collectively knowing the practices of shamanistic people like these healers and then recording those practices, which have turned into primal medical theory. These healers are just what they are, there is no method to follow, and as a result their expression is almost impossible to characterize. It is beyond principle, cannot be taught. It is therefore aligned with primal medicine because, in the end, primal medicine cannot be taught either, it can only open what is naturally within as a deeply-felt interest in healing as a way of expression.

It must be pointed out that belief systems do play a role in medicine. In western ideas this is called the placebo effect. The placebo is really the belief in something which relaxes contraction and then an allowance of the body to heal. The belief in the practitioner, however, has caused huge problems throughout the history of medicine because it focuses very strongly on the practitioner being the key to the medical process. This hierarchical ideology is not part of the deeply ancient way of the shamans and the healers, this primal route is a pure science which is about a directing of the patient back to their own sense of being, it does not rely on a belief system and as a result is about freedom of the patient from the binds of a belief-based mentality. This is something that is actually lacking in most modern practices where belief is still a strong component in the process of a person being helped using placebo, which then ties the patient and practitioner together forever. Also it was part of the darker side of Shamanism, a kind of black-magic which was all about believing if you were "good" then no harm would come, but if you were "bad" then you would fall sick and die. So strong are these beliefs that they can cure or kill. The point is root medicine is beyond belief systems, it is really about freedom from the known and allowance of nature. The ancient theory simply shows the road back to this in the dynamics of pure observation. This therefore becomes the basis of treatment. Deviation from this into the modern mentality of individualism usually brings hierarchical ideas and as such a use of ancient tools such as power and control processes. In my experience this is very common.

Ancient Indian medicine, ayurvedic medicine

Ayurvedic medicine is the medicine of the ancient people of India, the Vedic peoples. This is possibly the oldest of all the classical medicines. The roots of this medicine still survive in the expressions of yoga and related forms of exercise practised all over the world by so many. Ayurvedic roots can also be seen in techniques such as massage, acupuncture, the use of aromatic oils, numerous cathartics, purgative healing therapies and herbal medicine. The understanding of herbs in healing is of fundamental importance in Ayurvedic medicine. Although the plethora of tools of medicine in India and China is vast, the nature of the climates is such that the temperate China will have more extreme variety of tools than that of India, which in general has a more constant climate. However, where India meets Tibet, again the medicine is adapted to the region. Tibetan medicine is a synthesis of Chinese and Indian medicine with some indigenous medicine. Climate shapes the people's bodily form and also the medicinal forms. The herbs and yogic healing therapies are closely tied to the climate of India, the heat especially, making them useful in this regard, but the principle at the root remains adaptive as it is energetically rooted. Tibetan medicine combines Chinese and Indian ideas to form a single unit, expressing how the roots of medicine can all be joined very easily under the same expression. An Indian doctor may prescribe different medicine from a Chinese doctor, but the effect will bring about the same overall change and the root unity and base are the same; these are simply different expressions of the very same ancient track.

Ancient Greek medicine

Not much of ancient Greek medicine from the time of Aristotle and Hippocrates is practised, although many doctors still swear the Hippocratic Oath when joining the profession. Greek folk-remedies tell a story of medicine similar to that of shamanic ideology and belief systems. It is likely that Greek medicine originated in Egyptian/Babylonian regions and times. Usually, Greek medicine is considered to have four "elements" or energetic qualities/phases of nature relating to all of life, but the fifth "element" is more ancient and part of the heritage of the medicine, relating back to the Pythagoreans. This ties up strongly with both the Indian and Chinese 5 phase or element expression of energy in the east. A systemized form of medicine was developed in Greece and had Greek culture been allowed to prosper without interference, systemized medicine would have been bound to flourish. However, unlike China and India, which have their roots in prehistoric times, the Greek civilization was conquered by the Romans (around 170 BC) - right when the clearest insights into medicine were developing globally. This means that the Greek lineage of understanding was scattered in part. In China, however, there was enough time to formulate classical medicine to clarity and without as much corruption or influence from invading forces, although there was turmoil within China itself. The Greeks were moving towards this understanding and their ancient texts are similar to those around the Taoist-Confucians in China, when texts of shamanistic folk medicine began being systemized and a "Classical" art form was being created.

The basis of Greek culture and medicine also led to astrological studies (as is also the case in China and India) and an understanding of the personality and body via the heritage of the cosmos. It also led to a plethora of different remedies using the plants and medicines of the Greek region. Massage, aromatherapy, cupping and techniques for the healing of the body were used in the spas and bath-houses of Rome and have direct connection with Greek ideas. They were likely to have been the beginnings of hydrotherapy techniques which spread over the Western world at that time, involving drinking and using natural spring waters for numerous cures and remedies. There are similar stories all over the world when shamanism died a death, in civilizations like the Egyptian, Mayan, Incan and others. They were either overthrown by "civilization", or shamanism became a corrupted power tool, and so the medicine of the ancients was lost or misplaced and never formed a root medicine system. In England it was the same with the Druids, their medicine has perhaps been handed down through folk medicine in the form of the famous *Culpeper's Herbal* text, which contains some of the old remedies, the background sense of which have been lost in the past.

Ancient medicine is dying. There is just a handful of people worldwide who are interested in reclaiming the broad view of medicine. Just as the indigenous tribes are dying out, the pre-historic instinctive intuition is seen as an old relic or an archaeological issue, to be replaced by a computer program or a theoretical view from the individual's mind. Like a tree, if the roots die, the medicine is lost, and so it is important to keep it alive, which is what this book expresses. We are speaking, of course, not just about medicine here, but of our essential life force, as it is about Oneness.

2. Name-changing medicine of the "New - Age"; losing perspective

Therapeutic theories within this category have undergone drastic name changes, often due to marketing reasons and attempts to highlight various stylists of the original root medicine. Some modern therapies can be traced back to a traditional origin, while others, despite their being packaged to *look* traditional, are much more recent. You only have to scratch the surface to discover this. Like most reproductions, they are very seldom anything as whole as the original view clarity, but have a personal intention at their root whether acknowledged or unconscious. The therapeutic theories of the "New Age" include those we might think to be very traditional, but a little research quickly reveals that what appears to be "traditional" and "old" has simply been packaged very cleverly and is quite a new product. We must also not confuse the idea that old is good - this is not the point and is inaccurate as there have been many side-steps in the history of Root medicine where individuals take precedence for a brief moment and then are seen to be limited and instinctual sense moves on. Classical root medicine does have a complete picture of things but one which has been fragmented more and more in recent times. As such, this category of the "New Age" medicines is no older than 200 - 300 years, in comparison with ten times that for the root medicine from which these disciplines came.

This category often includes therapies that have been around for fewer than a hundred years. This shows the generations of collective recognition for the approaches and the fact that there is the empirical instinctual knowledge of thousands of generations in ancient medicine, relative to the very small numbers that have used the newer medicines. This is not about good and bad, it is just the facts. All the following therapies have to some degree or another moved or developed away from the root of the ancient energetic medicine. They have either become stylized, personalized, or do not adhere to the fundamental principles of the source entirely, but see only a portion of this, a bit like seeing a view through a tube rather than with just the naked eye.

Traditional Chinese Medicine (TCM) and the numerous styles of acupuncture, herbal medicine, and massage

It may be surprising to see TCM included here, as those who have studied very hard and spent years involved in TCM and other acupuncture styles are often adamant that they have the true and original picture. Most of the last ten years of my life have been spent unravelling the truth of this. I was lucky enough to connect to people who understood and could clearly differentiate useful information from obscure and I was directed to read the material focused in acknowledging the root of this problem. TCM is a style of root Chinese Classical Medicine derived from the classical material but missing the key to its understanding in the realms of massage, acupuncture, energy medicine healing, and, to a lesser degree, herbal medicine. Although much of the information is there, it is mixed about in such a way that the student practitioner has difficulty focusing on the prime principle of healing - the deficient root of the pattern. The heritage that was energy medicine healing was destroyed by a history of looking away from energy medicine, beginning as early as the first Emperor of China (259 BC - 210 BC). This reached a crescendo with Mao Zi Tong's presence in China during the Cultural Revolution of the 1940s to 1970s. As a result, TCM is a mauled and fragmented expression of what classical medicine used to be. (See: Fruehauf H. (1999)).

Some aspects of the ancient tradition are still within the material, but not everything, and in fact the most important aspects and simplicity of unified theory are still missing. TCM still uses all the various disciplines of healing that classical medicine does, but often in a coarser way. For example, the use of electro-acupuncture was introduced and it is common for acupuncture to be used in connection with modern bio-chemical medicine and innovations. After the Han Dynasty in China acupuncture and massage came to be used to treat the exterior body, they were increasingly considered to be less useful than herbs, and herbs were considered almost wholly to treat the inner body. Today, the pervasive perception is that acupuncture does not deeply affect the inner body as much as herbs do - and vice-versa - the idea of a whole and unified system is, largely forgotten in China. There are of course numerous styles of acupuncture. The list is endless - what follows is just a small sampling:

- Toyohari - a Japanese style which is the formulation of Kodo Fukushima

- Kiiko Matsumoto's acupuncture style - another prominent practitioner's style of treatment

- Manaka style acupuncture

- Stems and Branches theory and style of acupuncture

- The 6 Climate Qi school of herbal medicine (and
- acupuncture) of lineage to Wang Bing; 762AD

- Numerous schools of herbal styles - such as the Wen Bing or hot disease treatments

- Family style acupuncture (often a family of practitioners treating in their own way over generations, but clearly their own approach)

- Medical acupuncture - a form of treatment designed by modern medical doctors focusing on nerve stimulation

- Dry needling - a form a acupuncture often done by physiotherapists, chiropractors, and osteopaths not trained in classical understanding but using acupuncture, locally based on ideas of "myo-fascial and nerve-release trigger points";

this also includes trigger-point acupuncture

- Korean hand acupuncture - points are stimulated on the hand only
- Ear acupuncture - points are stimulated on the ear only

All of these are driven by organizations of individuals creating ideas of what acupuncture is, putting it in a box and offering it to practitioners - the tools are limited in so far as the theory of each individual style allows. There was, however, one school in Japan in the 1940s, the Keiraku Chiryo, or meridian therapy school, which had no theory other than to decipher and practise in the classical way. This is perhaps one of the last in the lineages from the ancient way of treating with acupuncture, yet even within this school there is deep fragmentation. Today, worldwide, only a handful of practitioners practise classical herbal medicine and acupuncture. There may be a few in China and there are a few in Japan, but in the west there are almost none.

TCM and the other various styles are neither good nor bad, but they are awkward, often caught between modern individualism and technology, with aspects of the ancient all mixed together in different ratios. The practitioners following these disciplines inevitably get restricted by trying to fit the shoes of the practitioner or practitioners they are attempting to emulate, rather than understanding the principles and expressing their own style - which is the ideology of Ikeda Masakazu, the main proponent of classical medicine worldwide and a standard-bearer of its acceptance and non-dual nature. What can be said is that TCM and other styles do help patients to find some way towards health again, but often the guidance of the practitioner is not able to really go all the way back to the heart of the problem. This is usually because the practitioner is blocked somewhere down the line in his/her contact with the root of the simple unity of the various syndromes and treatment perspectives, unable to see the whole broad picture of the issues at hand. This kind of stylism, often under the guise of unity and harmony, is actually within itself highly individualized and "cliquey," and it limits itself as a result. In the end, this restricts the natural flow of energy and of course this ideology is passed on to the patient, who accepts or rejects it, depending on their own senses. Often practitioners of these kinds of therapies will find that they draw a certain type of patient; it is the style itself that is drawing those patients to it. In a way, it is the "ghost" of the individual who created the style that they are attempting to wield. This of course makes things difficult, especially if one's own expression isn't very similar to that of the originator. Root medicine completes these styles and sees them as one. This is often difficult for these practitioners to appreciate, as they can be almost religious in their position of supremacy, but in the end they often arrive at it themselves, i.e. they practise and let go of theory altogether.

Shiatsu and Tuina

Shiatsu was originally part of the spectrum of Oriental classical medicine in the form of massage. This technique uses massage as a single therapy, and it can be a specialization dependent on the practitioner, although they may naturally also like other external therapies like acupuncture and moxibustion which are all really different exterior tools. Herbal medicine almost requires a different kind of person to investigate it, nevertheless massage is very much an aspect of Foundational tools of medicine. Shiatsu theory however, was conceived fifty years ago in Japan. Using a few of the numerous techniques of An-massage, classical meridian massage, Shiatsu focuses on the meridians and effects change by the feel and sensitivity of the practitioner, restoring good energetic flow down the meridians. Unfortunately, the lacking of the root classical theory means that diagnosis and treatment have numerous styles, like acupuncture has, notably, Masunaga style or "Zen Shiatsu," Endo style, Namakoshi style, and Yamamoto style, from the various Japanese practitioners who treated using massage. Interestingly, in China a similar thing happened to the original An-massage healing form. Tuina is one of the numerous techniques (the ones commonly missing from shiatsu in fact!) for massage. Generally, it focuses not on the meridians but on the tissues in between and horizontal to the lateral meridians. These tissues/meridians are called luo-meridians and are the main focus of tuina for clearing excess from the channels and restoring harmony through strong and direct pressure. The two techniques simply show the expressions of the different peoples of Japan and China. The Japanese approach of shiatsu is the yin of tuina, which is yang in comparison. Together they form a whole. They need to join together again or understand the nature of An-massage, which incorporates all technique into ancient principles of bodywork therapy.

There was no differentiation of the massage techniques until relatively recently. Again, the lack of theoretical foundation results in the diagnosis for tuina being based on an herbal medical outlook (i.e., TCM theory) of the body and meridians, and in shiatsu there is often either an individual stylistic approach (e.g., Masunaga's shiatsu) or modern nervous system ideas (e.g., Namkoshi shiatsu), which get in the way of direct contact with the patient. Amatsu, a form of very active and more forceful shiatsu combined with some of the practices of bone-setters, is used in the martial arts of Ninjitsu in Japan. The bone-setting arts and "osteopathic" manoeuvres would all have been considered part of An-massage, and the healing and effect on the meridians.

Sotai

Sotai (meaning "to manipulate the body") technique was derived from Classical oriental medicine by Keizo Hashimoto. It is another aspect of the full tool-kit of classical medicine. Sotai is a form of physical therapy where assisted exercises of tension-relaxation help to balance the activity in meridians. The same problem occurs here in that it is never clearly connected to the ancient approach and is limited to the style of the practitioner whose approach one is learning. Furthermore, it is just one approach, and this limits the practitioner to one tool. This is not a problem if one has the base theory to manipulate this tool, but without ancient principles this is impossible, so it tends to be used for symptomatic relief.

Seitai (Noguchi Seitai) and Sei-Kai (Akinobu Kishi)

Seitai, means "body manipulation/ movement" or "ordering the body" is an umbrella term for many not formally grouped body-manipulation arts in Japan. Practices like Shiatsu or Sotai and even forms of bone-setting and osteopathic-like manipulation, if they had not been formally regulated, could come under the broader banner of Seitai. However Harchika Noguchi's form or Seitai is now most often associated with the term which has only really been around since the 1920s -1940s. Hence Noguchi's Seitai, a term used only by his students not by him, is what we will discuss here. Noguchi's understanding was based fundamentally in sensitive instinctive sense that perfectly reflected the Classics of Oriental medicine, but unlike many of his proponents he rejected modern concepts of the body and went right to the root of Classical medicine. In his process he came into contact with the spontaneous self-healing responses of the body, and a triggering of this. As a result he begin to explore techniques and exercises that are common to Tao-Yin or "naturally led movement" / self-massage which are simply naturally-felt stretching and non-form expression of the body. This instinctual sensitivity is the foundation of all medicine as it is the body's own unique way to resolve problems. Noguchi was a non-interventionist and focused on non-action as the basis for healing something which is the foundation to all healing of the ancient world, the yin perspective, which is quickly falling from modern view. This ties up with the more modern expression such as "Authentic movement" formed from the foundational philosophy within Carl Jung's investigations into ancient understanding. Seitai can be considered in total alignment with the nature of Classical medicine but as it is based on one person's investigations, namely Noguchi, it does render a kind of segregation in its use because it is hard for people to see its roots rather than its author. This is probably much more to do with the people surrounding Noguchi than Noguchi himself. As with many who are clearly reaching the roots of medicine it is usually their fore-runners and students who lose clarity and turn something that is calling to the Oneness of the universal into a hierarchically-dominated strait-jacket. The reason this is associated with the "New-age" ideology is simply because of its focus in a single advocate, but actually Noguchi's work is deeply foundational.

A proponent of Noguchi's work and a long term teacher of Shiatsu formed his own realization this core of medicine, Akinobu Kishi's Sei-ki (Sei-ki approximately means "Regulating of energy to natural-authenticity"). Borrowing much from Noguchi's understanding of the body and spontaneous responses of healing Kishi's work continues the connection of reaching deeply and sensitively into the heart of the ancient root of the timeless energetic medicine and its profound nature. Kishi draws all the elements of the ancient forms of An-massage back to its true origin and as such his work is a vital resource.

Reiki

Reiki, which means "mysterious atmosphere or feeling" is hugely popular and is most probably derived from the eastern healing arts of Qi Gong. Qi Gong is a foundational expression of the healing arts of primal medicine. If taught in a way that is not forceful or aggressive, it is a direct expression of the root medicine . Those who practise it on a deep level will very often be intuitively practising primal medicine. Reiki is energy healing without the root principles, and as a result it is utterly full to bursting with individualism and ideology which is a product of its originator's stylistic idea of what healing is - developed in 1922 by Japanese Buddhist Mikao Usui. Reiki has been practised for eighty years or so.

More recently other individuals have formed their own explanation and hands-off healing methodologies, for example, Re-Connective healing is the trademark of Dr. Eric Pearl. Dr. Pearl states that his therapeutic approach is "natural medicine" but also that it is a new medicine that he has discovered, (Pearl E., 2001). Although Eric Pearl and numerous others have a deep healing gift, very often they are the ones to formulate styles of practice like his, which are their expression in the world. Yet, because they do not have all-inclusive root principles at their base, they are almost impossible for other people to access and know in themselves as one's direct expression of instinctual healing.

Reiki theory focuses on balancing Chakra energy regions through the feeling and sensitivity of the practitioner, which is very important and is grounded in deep intuitive sense. (Please note that Chakras are no different to any other expression of the energetic energy regions of the body in Chinese medicine or any of the ancient understanding, just a different word for the same thing - aspects of expressions of the energy field of the human being.) However, the practice is often less effective due to a lacking of principles at the root of treatment, which results in a confused direction in treatment.

Intuitive healers know what to do without intellectually knowing what to do, and if one is able to access this kind of sense, then this is a purely natural expression which will always adhere to the root principles. In many ways the reason to "study" is only to gain insight into this feeling, no one can "attune you" you are already attuned to everything, it is simply a matter of trusting this process, which is something that often seems to come with a big price tag or a process of "humbling oneself" to a self-righteous "powerful" teacher one has to be "under". This is not medicine, respect is to acknowledge what is, no more and no less. Medicine is free and has no hierarchy and is already your own instinct. The root principles are simply charted expression of a natural, innately known sense of heat and cold (at a fundamental level. If one isn't able to connect to this intuition immediately, root principles help to initiate this process. Reiki is therefore important as it has interest in energetic connection, it resonates with a Oneness and realizes the intuitive base, much like all forms of "spiritual healing". However unless the practitioner can instinctually find their way through to the intuitive only, and the grounded sense of reality in treatment, it can become too narrowly associated to its originator's belief system.

Reflexology

Reflexology has its roots in Indian and Classical Chinese Medicine, but it has been stylized, and the principles have been substituted for "new" ideas regarding the anatomical relation to the sole of the foot, which was originally energetic ideology. This may seem trivial, even just re-naming, but as we can see, with re-naming also comes the loss of the connection to the energetic sea in which the foot-treatment originated. Reflexology is based on pressure-pain responses with the soles of the feet. Different regions of the feet are associated with different energetic systems of the body, but often these are attributed to organs specifically in the more modern interpretations, which do not often consider the energetic network associated with each organ system. This treatment is very effective, no matter what the condition, because the focus is on the feet - the main sources of the prime deficiency in energy flows. The lowest energy area in the modern human is in the feet, in almost all cases. Nearly all cases of healing require energy to move back down to the feet and away from the upper body; heat rises, so the connection with the earth is naturally deficient. However, reflexology is also *limited* because it focuses only on the sole of the foot. It is feet-focused, just as Korean hand acupuncture or ear acupuncture are focused on one body part, seeing and affecting all other regions of the body through that one part. Someone with their lower legs amputated would not be able to have reflexology in the traditional way, and so this limits the situation. Root medicine is totally adaptive because it doesn't look at the specific regions of the body; instead, it looks at the foundational or root issues which can be seen in any region of the body. What has happened, is that the branches have not been focused on the whole tree. Reflexology and the other therapies see the hologram of the body through one part, so are simply a part of the whole.

Indian head massage

This is another therapy that focuses on a part in order to treat the whole. Indian head massage was once part of a full-body, healing massage which has now been fragmented into parts. Treatment consist of various massage techniques applied to the head, neck and shoulders. It is not as energetically "safe" as reflexology is because it has the tendency to draw up energy to the head. Indian head massage, on its own, can often cause too much stimulation to the upper body. It is useful sometimes, in the right condition, to relax the head and shoulders. However, with no other stimulation to the lower body, the opening of the upper body provides symptomatic relief only, meaning that the lower body is the place where energy needs to be drawn to calm the body and anchor the energy. Opening up the upper body does release tension, but similarly to other cathartic methods this is homeopathic, it draws up and out but doesn't anchor down and in, or strengthen the deficient root; this is because it is part of a full spectrum of massage treatment without which its theoretical view is partial.

If aligned with the root principles, then all of these focused, one-point approaches could join together to treat people as a whole. Each practitioner resonates with a different part of the body, so if all those people got together, the whole body of a patient could be treated. There's nothing wrong with specialization in an area of the body, the only problem is seeing it exclusively. The other approach is to see the whole pattern and focus only on one area - the one most in need - and let nature take its course. Root medicine aims to be efficient and direct, so the ability to diagnose the appropriate therapy is key, this makes for efficient healing. As in nature, nothing is wasted.

Swedish massage, sports massage, remedial massage

The various forms of massage, which generally use oil, originated in Greek and Roman spas, hot baths, and places of healing. Today, much of the energetic understanding of these times has been put aside and replaced with a Western anatomical and physiological view of the body. These types of massage tend to be deep and penetrating. The massage of Caucasian people is very different from that of other races, due to differences in constitution. The skin of Caucasian people needs regular treatment to help open and close the pores of the skin as this process can easily become impaired and blocked. This is not the case for all races. This massage treatment is often conjoined with a steam treatment and sauna. They are very much focused on relaxing tension and smoothing out excesses. It is totally contra-indicative for cold and weak patients, which restricts this treatment to people who need its strength and opening/catharsis. Also, the reason such aggressive techniques are required is because of ineffective use of the body, with either too much exercise or unnatural body movement that creates injuries. In addition, lack of exercise results in the accumulation of heat and tension, necessitating a practitioner to get the body moving. This obviously doesn't change anything in relation to a person's health.

To be truly remedial, the practitioner that understands the basic pattern of heat or cold and knows how to prescribe the right exercise, or rest, to help the patient in a direction away from requiring relaxation by the masseur is really aiding health instinct. Otherwise, the patient becomes an addict to the process, which does no good to anyone involved. Many of the so-called remedial treatments, because they have lost the foundational theory, turn into treatments of the service and beauty industry which is not what this was originally about. Medicine isn't a service, it is more of a provider of direction, a signpost back to the instinctual. This must be clearly understood. Beauty treatments of the superficial kind, i.e., working on the skin for the skin's sake rather than garnering beauty via internal health, must be clearly differentiated from medicine.

Hot stones treatment

In the last few years, a re-interest in hot stone therapy has emerged. It finds its origin in Japanese and North American Indian medicine, as well as other ancient medicines from around the world. Hot stones, warmed to a little higher than body temperature, are placed on energy centre/acu-points, and stones are used in massage treatments to release tissue tension. This is a very useful form of massage and a treatment similar to that of moxibustion, *if* the practitioner understands the principles. Otherwise, the use of hot stones can actually cool a patient down, by over-using them and thereby inducing sweating. Also a very warm or high-tension patient can be made worse if hot stones are placed around the heart and head. This is obvious to the principles of common-sense which is root yinyang theory, but not to those who are not involved with intuitively sensing the body and are only following protocol and associating the treatment with beauty. Hot stones can be a powerful tool if used with the background sensitivity. Cold stones have also been used and these are much more energetically damaging to those who are already cold. A simple and obvious intuitive response is all that is needed: "common sense" is the key. However, to use common sense is to come from a foundational perspective and root oneself, in knowing cold from heat, yin from yang.

EFT (Emotional Freedom Technique)

EFT developed out of a combination of psychotherapy and an idea regarding the meridians of the body from Oriental medicine. Gary Craig, in the early 1990s, came up with the term EFT. The technique involves teaching the patient to tap areas of their body where "emotion" is said to be held. They then "let go" of the tensions in the body through this methodology. This is an interesting technique which does allow people to become more closely aware of the union of body and emotional feeling, which can be a link to instinctive self-awareness. The difficulty is that EFT is governed by a theory that has little interest in the root medicine in which the meridians were clearly known and originated from. As with kinesiology, the energetics of the body-spirit are not being understood and there is an attempt to Westernize them. As a result, although the technique can't do any damage, it may confuse the situation and doesn't allow for a meaningful realization of what is actually occurring. The idea of self-massage comes from ancient practices in all root medicine, including those with stretching and opening, like yoga, and those with energetic re-alignment, like Tao-Yin (naturally-led self-massage) and Qi Gong. These medicines are the foundation of this newer idea. Modern psychological theories do come close to energetic primal understanding (especially those associated with people looking towards a sense of Oneness like for example Carl Jung), however this is a partial view because it is being seen through an analytic process of the individual's western mind. EFT looks at symptoms in the emotions and strength area of suffering, as does commonly the psychotherapeutic process because it is in itself working with the mind which inevitably is the dis-ease, and so it inevitably becomes about catharsis of expression, rather than about the tonification deficiency at the root of the problem which will to some degree or another be connected to areas of weakness in body energy.

Overall one could say that cathartic treatments are very much the methodology of the Western world and tonification is the methodology of the Eastern world. This has much to do with constitutional differences between the peoples, however the understanding of the ancient world underpins both "ways" of working and therefore is not a one-for-all blanket method of treatment. When EFT is seen as part of energetic self-massage then its strength is broadened to see that catharsis is only one of the ways of treatment, and depending on the situation different things will be required.

Catharsis is all about the release of tension and exhaustion bringing about relaxation, tonification is purely about deep relaxation. Again it is the yin-deficient situations where cathartic action is often "wanted", however this can be come a pattern that doesn't change, catharsis being constantly used to release when tension gets to its limit. This is partially to do with the nature of the personality, however the curative aspect is never the catharsis itself but always its resolution into relaxation, the relaxation is the yin, the cure. The catharsis is always the activation, the irritant that reaches a peak, expresses and then forms relaxation. Once we see that both aspects are part of a whole we can see that for yang deficiency this would be inappropriate and not all westerners are yin-deficient all the time, this is just a constitutional tendency.

Applied kinesiology

Applied Kinesiology was founded in 1964 by George J. Goodheart, a chiropractor. Applied Kinesiology professes to balance the body through effecting neuromuscular points, energy points and lymphatic points over the body surface which are diagnostically indicated by a series of musculoskeletal tests called "muscle testing". The basic idea is that the patient's weaker areas should be strengthened and stronger areas weakened, in order to balance the body out. Kinesiological theory is a grand attempt at a combination of the ideas of western methodology/ physiology and Eastern oriental medicine. What it unfortunately does is to mix numerous methods together, to form a highly complex system. The problem is really that kinesiology attempts to take the "best of both worlds" point of view, which is actually to force aspects of the energetic wholeness into the western dualistic musculoskeletal and physiological function, fragmentary model. Although the system is very clever and ingenious, it is a composite idea of Ancient Eastern meets Western scientific which squashes the ancient meridian system into a Western framework of mental concepts of meridians and what they are. This is quite an attempt, but to get to the root it would require to let go of much of the modern mechanistic thinking and see what the original ancient material had to offer in and of itself. This would have rendered a broader perspective. The Kinesiological approach is interesting as it allows perhaps the modern-minded westerner to engage with an energetic idea, but it also skews the idea of what energetics is about, which needs to be let go of before a broader picture and a more inclusive model can be seen beneath.

This said, however, the process of diagnosis used in kinesiology called "muscle testing" is an ingenious method of testing the performance of muscle-meridian regions of the body in order to find the strongest and weakest in a given symptom situation of the patient's problem, be they more psychological or more physical in expression. It is commonly used for testing possible allergens, by introducing the food stuff or material of relevance to the body's energetic field, so it is touching the person's body or is close to it, then doing tests to see if the patient "wants it", showing muscular-energetic strength, or weakness if it is a poison to the body. One of the problems of this diagnostic technique from the broader primal or unified perspective, is that tendon-muscle tissues although they do have association to each meridian are always associated with the meridian system of the liver and gallbladder organs in Classical medicine. Hence what seems like a holistic system was not invented by the ancients because they would have known they would only be testing one expression of energy throughout the body, which is why it would not have been relevant, other than as only part of a treatment process. The ancient methods of diagnosis incorporate all the levels of tissues in the body and do not focus on just one. This is not to say its therapists do not help to heal patients, but I would say that this is due to the therapist, not the working theoretical model. In its incorporation of ancient Eastern aspects the whole is not seen so the view is limited.

Rolfing, structural integration, bowen technique

Rolfing is a technique of "structural integration" (designed by Ida Pauline Rolf in 1950's) which, often with deep massage, strongly treats the fascial, tendon sheath-like tissues of the body found most concentrated around the joints of the musculo-skeletal system. It is based on the fascial system of the body being the focus of treatment. The Bowen technique, from the work of Tom Bowen (1916 - 1982), is a technique that uses very light pressure around the joints of the body. Both healers got brilliant results, and few know the way the original creators of these techniques did it, but they are now a "handed down" method to the next generation. Again, if seen in context, these techniques are useful and interesting, but the limitations of such styles are acute; they are mechanistically focused often in the fascial tissues and can easily become "routines" because root philosophy is not in place in order to see the work in context. However all practices can be routine if the practitioner is not one with the process, which is why energetic understanding is so vital at the root. There are now numerous systems of "Structural Integration" all from the Ida Rolf original umbrella, some more holistic and mind-body focused than others. Notably is the work of Joseph Heller (creating the school of "Heller Structural Integration").

Cranio-sacral osteopathy

As differentiated from general osteopathy, cranio-sacral work was derived from osteopathy but requires higher sensitivity and engagement of the practitioner's senses. Cranio-sacral osteopathy focuses on the cranium and the sacrum. It helps the body to relax and release tension through natural movements of energy in the patient's body. The practitioners help these energies to flow naturally and intervention is minimal. This is based on work by William Sutherland (1898 - 1900), who formed the ideas around osteopathy. Though Sutherland was not specifically labelled as an energetic healer and explained things in terms of osteopathic ideas, he was very close in his expression of energetic ideas, calling the pulsation that is a sensory-felt experience by the practitioner as "the breath of life", which comes as close as is possible to one of the translations of Qi, in Chinese, as "breath". In Oriental medicine, there is a focus on the area of the bladder meridian which runs down the whole back and neck and regulates all the other meridians. Essentially it is the whole back of the body. It is perhaps the most vital meridian on the body for healing (although as the Shiatsu teacher Michel Rose said "there is only one meridian!" meaning the whole of the body and also all of existence), and it is always treated, no matter what the pattern presenting is. As a form of relaxation therapy, this works very well and moves close to a form of hands-on healing. However, the mechanistic approach, which is common to osteopathy is still present, so this blocks the possibility of focusing on the whole body instead of just on the cranium and sacrum, which is fragmentary. Cranio-sacral therapy itself is without universal principles, in that it is not an energetic-based ideology, so the focus is on mechanics rather than sensing intuitively. However, the skilled therapist moves into regions which can no longer be called "osteopathic." I am being specific to the theories and ideas of Sutherland here and am well aware that numerous practitioners in this field have expanded into energetic medicine. This is always the case, as we can see with all the therapies, when the practitioner's intuitive sense takes over from the theoretical approach they learned, which is usually highly individual or limited; they move into an unlimited space which is the exact same intuition that primal medicine mirrors in theory as well as in practice. The theory is simply more data, but a directing of oneself back to instinct, it is a theory in fact that ends the requirement for theory, books that end books.

Again this book is looking at the use and limitation of different theoretical systems and how they often in the modern renditions of ancient medicine start to separate off from the whole picture which is really a kind of tension held in practice. When this tension lets go and there is no more "personal presence" of either the theory of the originator or of the personal ideas, then something else happens which is what is represented in intuitive primal medicine. The process of being involved in any and all therapeutic traditions is absolutely fine, but it must be seen within the context of what it is; when there is theoretical limitation this will always hamper the experience of both patient and practitioner. Root medicine is both your unique expression and also the music that flows this instrument. It is purely instinctive at root. When there is theory involved things become complicated and belief systems start to creep in, as do hierarchical ideas and the attempt to claim power or control over something. This is simply fear, whomever it is from, a "high-up" teacher or "lowly" student or patient, the problem here is still the same old passing-on of the dis-ease of separation.

Alexander technique

This methodology is a form of taught practice for natural movement designed by F. Matthias Alexander in the 1890s.

Alexander was an actor, and in order to correct his vocal chords, he found ways of standing and operating in movement that allowed his body to be firmly grounded yet natural (Alexander F.M., 1932). He had found through his own body sense some of the techniques of Qi Gong and Tai Chi and the plethora of ancient exercise arts, and if he had looked into it, or this information been available to him at the time, he would have found his roots and would have rooted his theory into principles which are much more complete and universal than his theories could have been, seeing only from his perspective. However, in quite a mechanical way, his therapy and expression are close to root ideas. Energetic understanding and yinyang principles could help to make more fluid his mechanism, something that is possible to go beyond for some practitioners who are coming from instincts. It is often subject to hierarchical problems and nuances of difficulty as to "what Alexander meant by ... X," which is the hallmark of any tradition based on a single person rather than on universal principles. Primal medicine isn't rooted here, but the Alexander Technique shows direction towards it.

Feldenkrais method

Moshé Feldenkrais (1904 - 1984) moving in his own direction, but of similar interest, formed The Feldenkrais Method, a deeply considered and sensitive form of self-healing, which moves strongly towards the ancient root philosophies in their methodology and focus on awareness of body in a similar way to that of the Alexander Technique and Sotai above. The Feldenkrais method is very much about body awareness and moving to a place of unrestricted and intuitive body sense, an "awareness through movement forming "integration" of the body. Again the limitation is always the focus of the perspective and/or originator's signature outlook of the approach, rather than unified language of energetics in Root medicine. The problem in many of the therapeutic techniques associated with an individual's name is that one needs to overcome the style of the originator to get to the root understanding and then find the natural expression of the essence through you.

These practices and also similar integrative what has been known as "mind-body-spirit" practices, like "bio-dynamic" bodywork therapy (inspired by the work of Rudolph Steiner), move very close to energetic medicines and those practising these systems are easily able to understand Root medical practice, usually because the founders of these techniques drew from ancient sources in their work. Many of the "new age" therapies are interesting composite expressions of individuality and root principles, you get both the teacher's signature and the ancient understanding rolled into one. Very often this is the case with practices but inevitably one has to find a way to see the principles through the individualistic limitations or one will inevitably follow the teacher's limits and not explore oneself from the background understanding or find one's own way to engage with the issues. Very often body-based therapies fail to interact or see the importance of the spirit quality and become too mechanical and physical and locked within this way of thinking. Those who focus on the spirit can very easily be drawn into the mind and be focused very much on mentally-derived mechanisms for health which cannot be found at that plain. The body-spirit is a unity which cannot be broken and all aspects need to be responded to, some may respond better to body, others better to spirit, some patients being more body or more spirit-orientated by nature of personality. If based in classic principles, diagnosis allows one to view the whole and know what's best for a person. The theory of medicine of each of these individual styles tells a story of a person's nature and way, but this is one light amongst the whole spectrum. To be influenced by one light does not allow us to see one's "own" necessarily, so it is useful to be aware of this when considering these bodies of work.

Homeopathy

Of all the modern Western-based therapies, this is probably the most holistic and most rooted in universal energetic principle. However, very often this principle is not adhered to, and because of this practitioners of other therapies are not clearly understood by the homeopath in relation to his/her own practice and its contextual benefits/limitations. Classical homeopathic principle understood and developed by Christian Friedrich Samuel Hahnemann, 1755 - 1843, forming the basis of modern homeopathy, has been used for thousands of years within primal medicine as a way to clear symptomatic issues from the body, although not in the way homeopathy, as a subject on its own, has formed. It is never seen as a root treatment, as the root is always a deficiency. Homeopathy works by finding the most poisonous substance for a person at a particular time in their life, something that would make all of their symptoms worse. Complex homeopathy created in the last 40 - 50 years by Dr. Hans Heinrich Reckeweg, M.D. in Germany uses numerous substances to provide the exact match of symptoms to patients, whereas what is called "classical" homeopathy which is similar to how Hahnemann would have practised, just uses one at a time. In either case, the trace energy of the poison is required, so the poison is diluted up to a million times or more. The water that is used to dilute has only a trace of the energetic blueprint of the original substance, but this whiff of energy is all that is needed to increase the symptoms - just a little - in the patient. When this happens, the hope is that the patient's system has the ability to self-correct the balance, by going in the opposite direction of the effect of the poison and cathartically removing its symptoms, as well as the trace energy of the poison, from the system.

Homeopathy, therefore, is categorized as a form of catharsis within foundational ideology, nothing more and nothing less. If this is acknowledged fully by homeopaths, it would be easy to see why using allopathy (treatment of opposites) alongside homeopathy would be counter to its effectiveness. When within Foundational medicine homeopathic principle is part of a branch or secondary treatment for local issues, or as part of a course of treatment aimed to treat the deficient root of the problem through strengthening after catharsis of one kind or another has been used; which would occur (in this order) mainly in acute situations often involving heat. Chronic situations which tend to move towards cooling of the body in old age or severe sickness and tiredness require the allopathic approach far more than homeopathic. (Please note whenever I am using allopathic in this book I am never referring to bio-medicine which calls itself "allopathic medicine" without understanding the root energetics of this term). The primary fundamental healing is always allopathic strengthening of the deficiency. Hence, modern homeopathy theory is very broad, but in a narrower view than the full spectrum of root ideology is principally missing the concept of deficiency. As a result, it is very often not practised within a spectrum of modalities that could make its understanding focused and useful. Another problem is lack of clarity about the ideology of the "strength" of the homeopathic substance being used. A "strength" dose is often associated with the highest levels of dilution. The way this can be understood in primal medicine terms is as follows:

Low dilution =
more physical
effect (yin)

High dilution =
more subtle
energetic effect
(yang)

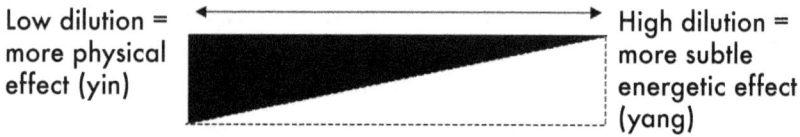

The higher the dilution, the more the energetic becomes yang. When expanded, it affects the immaterial aspects of the system more than the material. This can cathartically change a mood instantly. The effect is more and more immediate with the higher dilutions and there is less and less effect on physical issues. The effect is more on mood and emotional subtleties. Higher dilutions are best for symptoms that are acute. The lower dilutions, similar to those that Hahnemann himself would have used, are more effective on physical ailments and move towards poisonous cathartics and irritants. Again, this is not about judging different therapeutics, but rather about looking at them from the perspective of the root medicine from which they were born. The idea is to provide root to allow for contextualized, understood healing and a way to use these tools most appropriately for each individual patient, or better, to see that the tool is only a means, not the end of treatment. In homeopathy we see an energetic understanding, an acceptance of universality of energy but a limitation within this not to see the allopathic aspect of the whole picture, this is the yang without the yin so to speak.

Bach flower remedies

Bach flower remedies are usually used to treat high-tension situations or emotional pressures and tension. Edward Bach was obviously an intuitive healer and keenly understood the human in relation to plants. Intuitively, he chose flowers as the key to emotional connection, which ties in directly with the root medicine use of flower heads to affect the heart and head regions

- the seats of emotional expression, particularly in situations of acute anxiety. He then proceeded to use the flower essences diluted to trace in alcohol. As with homeopathic medicine, Bach remedies are at a dilute energetic level effect, but unlike homeopathy Bach remedies are allopathic and so balance out emotional disturbances which are self-prescriptive, particularly in acute situations. This is easily and effortlessly tied to root medicine, it is using yinyang balancing to a useful degree, and it is used for acute situations, such as his famous "rescue remedy". The simplicity of the flower remedies makes them useful, although other herbs and understanding, not just of flowers, makes them a part of the bigger picture of herbal medicine.

Aromatherapy

The use of aromatic oils is particularly key in Indian, Middle Eastern and Greek medicine, and to a lesser degree in Chinese medicine. Similar to the way herbal medicine works, with aromatherapy a particular oil is applied to the skin in order to be drawn into the blood circulation and then have certain effects. When this therapy maintains its energetic roots, and so energetic effect of the herbs used, this is a very foundational tool of medicine. This would have originally been part of herbal medicine and akin to massage as well. However, herbal medicine would not have used only aromatic oil-based medicine, because all medicines can be applied through the skin when the mouth cannot be used for absorption. The energetic of the herbs, if known and understood by the practitioner, can be used to effect changes in heat and cold in alignment with the patient's situation. The skin is the primary way of treating here, so heating will cause sweating, and cooling down the skin will cause the whole body to cool down. It is also possible to use less pungent herbs than those which would cause sweating and in fact just warm the blood - this has a more tonifying effect.

However in general, aromatic herbs have "aroma". This means they are pungent. As a result, they are commonly associated with a form of cathartic release, an opening out of the body rather than putting energy in. For certain patients that are over-chilled this is generally inappropriate. Again, adherence to foundational principles of diagnosis would greatly help to root this practice. Today, ideas and theories of Western biochemistry are limiting this practice, as the focus has switched from the energetics of it to the molecules and chemistry involved.

Hopi candles

Hopi candles are another aspect of a traditional medicine that has been isolated probably for commercial purposes. The Hopi candle is not, as many people believe, specific to the Hopi Indian tribe, but it was used by people of this region and also in China, as a method for preventing and treating ear problems. It could said to be akin to a kind of moxibustion technique of a particular kind. A hollow candle made from a sheet of hessian dipped in beeswax is placed on the ear and lit at the top. A mild suction effect occurs through the channels of the ear and helps to clear blockages and prevent infections from moving closer to the ear drum and causing damage. This can prevent and resolve ear problems in some cases, and it is also very relaxing and calming, as the sound of the candle's suction is warm and soothing. It is therefore a highly focused treatment but a general one as well. Little harm can be done with this treatment if used properly. It is really a symptomatic treatment, but if one knows the diagnostics of the pattern, one can tell if the treatment will be effective before it is applied. For example, if the ear block is due to tension and heat in this region, it is better to do exercise to clear the problem. If, however, it is due to weakness and deficiency, then the candles can work very well. When the body is too tense, tight, and hot, it won't work so well; it works better when the patient is cold, deficient, and weak. This is known through primal principles, simply acknowledging the theoretical base of cold-heat yinyang we can connect the energetic root to all these various healing tools which would otherwise have belief systems and dogmatism associated with them applied simply as a blanket treatment for a huge number of problems.

Modern feng shui

Feng Shui means "wind and water" in Chinese, it is the ancient art of attunement of senses to the environment. I am including classical Feng Shui as part of primal medicine, even though this book is mainly about medicine of the interior body. Feng shui and related ideology from other parts of the ancient world seen in the ancient evidence of relation of human to natural energy such as the standing stone of the Druids, should be considered as medicine of the exterior or outer body-of-nature, the expanded body of the whole earth and sky. There is no separation between interior and exterior in all primal understanding of Oneness. In fact it is a major part of the difficulties we have today, based on individualism and separation from the world around us, that we do not see the unity of human with nature. This primary discrepancy is dis-ease itself.

While classical Feng Shui is now a rarity and is more akin today to the permaculture movement, where humans are looking to nature to direct their agricultural activities rather than trying to focus nature to do what they "want," modern Feng Shui has lost the classical base from which it was derived. Classical Feng Shui was deeply based in Taoism and it understood the total unity of nature with humans, similar to the way North American Indians feel about union with the land. In 1854 Chief Seattle said, (poetically rendered by Dr. Henry A. Smith):

*"Teach your children what we have
taught our children
-- that the earth is our mother. Whatever
befalls the earth befalls
the sons of the earth. If men spit upon the
ground, they spit upon
themselves. Whatever befalls the earth
befalls the sons of the
earth. Man did not weave the web of life,
he is merely a strand in
it. Whatever he does to the web, he does
to himself."*

*(Quote from: www.rainbowbody.net/
ongwhehonwhe/chiefsea.html)*

....which is what we are seeing today. There are films today
which express this same message, such as the James Cameron
film, Avatar. However, Feng Shui has been corrupted by the idea
that the city can be a place of harmony. The city is the capital of
all that goes against natural flow, so the use of Feng Shui in a
city is akin to eating organic food from New Zealand when you
live in London. The idea is about attempting to skew nature to
the modern ways of thinking, which is impossible because of
the nature of Oneness being all of everything, and so unable
to be grasped and manipulated. Classical Taoism directs people
back to ruralisation and union with nature, back to simplicity
rather than contempt for natural flows. Nature is the only place
in which Feng Shui can be used effectively. Considering the fact
that the environment is vital for humans on the earth, our natural
instincts will inevitably take us away from all that is dangerous,
noisy, polluting, and toxic - if we only listen to them. If we do not
do so now we will eventually be forced to, as a result of the end

of oil production and the climate change. In the end, it doesn't matter, it's simply a question of now or later. Nature has always been in the background and so in the end it becomes clear that this background is us - it is not separate from us. Feng Shui was originally designed to get our senses attuned to direction and placement of objects in the environment. It was about humans instinctually finding places where they could dwell, connected to and sustained by the earth.

Compasses and other tools were only methods for understanding the forms and shapes of the earth, as qualities of energy able to bring health and prosperity, or decay and energy-draining. Feng Shui directs us away from constructing buildings too close to one another and from building on the sides of volcanoes and on lines of earthquakes. Feng Shui directs humans to follow the seasons and to listen to nature rather than forcing themselves upon it. This is the true nature of Feng Shui. Painting an apartment red because it is best for greatly adding to its value is a modern fabrication of an ancient fundamental truth.

Crystal healing

Using crystals as a prime source of energy healing covers a huge number of different therapeutic principles. Akin to Feng Shui and other arts associated with the placement of energetic substances around the body, crystals have been used in the healing process since shamanic times. For thousands of years different rocks have been revered for their power and properties. Very often there is consensus about what the energetic effects of particular stones are and ideas of what one rock does and what another one does not. Some people can sense the energetic vibration, or in modern fragmented terms would be akin to magnetic fields, of rocks and crystals better than others, but their use in healing has long been known. However, as with herbal medicine, the right combinations are the ones that are best for you to be around at any one time, and these can change. This again is a diagnostic issue, so one can do it by trial and error, or literally see what is happening, sense the patient's condition, and connect this with the treatment. Magnet therapy is part of this very same ideology. There is nothing wrong with any of these expressions of energy. Let us look at their origin. How we can use them? How we can understand one another, not from an individualist's subjective view, but from something broader? Their origin is again found in the ancient understanding of the Oneness of yinyang or other such philosophy, which can be used to explore anything. The energetic "radiation" of stone is already quite cold in relation to that of humans. Therefore, on the grand scale, stones cool and calm the body. Hence, they are generally not applicable for very cold or deficient people, although I realize that there are some stones which are useful for this.

If we consider all materials to have an energetic effect, then all of life becomes part of the sea of energy, things aren't differentiated from one another, and it isn't just crystals that heal, but everything in every way. Healing isn't something that is performed, it is an allowance for a state of instinct to return, or a realization of Oneness to emerge from the background. No animal holds onto a sacred stone for the rest of its life, but animals may go to a spot of calm and quiet, where they can feel at peace when they need to. For example, they may do so if they are hurt, in order to experience a restful and inwards direction, rather than attending to the exterior. This is also the expression of Feng Shui and the arts of exterior placement, including acupuncture, though that uses metals instead of stones, which aids the process of directing outer energy inwards, so that we no longer need the treatment.

Modern astrology, divination and associated arts

Astrology may seem like a far cry from medicine, but understanding the spiritual essence of people can help in deep psychological ways to free them from great tension within. Ancient Astrology probably originated from shamanistic times. It has become more refined as time has gone on, but also fragmented. The ancient ways can help deep psychological issues and allow people to see themselves within a bigger context. This is true too of the I Ching and other divinatory expressions. These are the fundamentals of primal psychological-spiritual understanding - this was known and used by Carl Jung in his own treatment with patients, (Wilhelm R., 1968). The Divinatory arts are all considered aspects of Root medicine approaches, which would include what would today be termed "psychic" readings and intuitive readings of numerous kinds. There are, of course, people who are prone to make use of this understanding for purposes of financial gain or power and control, all human, worldly ideas, not the wild-nature that these feelings are sensed and drawn from. However this is the case with all things. The fact that mind and image are used a lot by these people, as well as those involved in hypnotics and other aspects of the ancient shamanism, means that they are more likely to be deluded and lost than the physical therapists who are generally more grounded, although the physical therapists tend not to acknowledge the benefits of the more ethereal systems.

Both are the different expressions of different people. The value of clarifying the mind is very ancient and so when connected to deep Primal intuitive sense, these practitioners always direct the person back towards their own instincts. They do not turn into opinionated oracles or soothsayers to be relied upon and rallied, but instead help to provide direction in times when mental confusion has deluded/dulled the senses. People with this sense and skill can so easily be confused and overrun by their emotions and ideas, it is very easy for a large egoic expression to emerge and for a person to be utterly locked into a particular fantasy, which is very much due to the mind-focused quality. When a person is really able to be free in this realm there is a deep awareness and grounded-ness of the body and lightness of the mind, there is a clear sense and open vessel of expression. This is rare in the modern age, usually people of high sensitivity in this way need to be in rural places and live in regions away from modern life to actually speak from truth without egoic formations developing due to the nature of the collective mental skewing of "civilization". Therefore these methodologies, at their best clarify and simplify, or at their worst add to and complicate the burden of a contracted consciousness.

Astrology is not about reading signs and living by them, it is about finding one's intuitive sense and re-connecting to what one knows about situations, without prescribed information. All of the divinatory and astrological arts have developed to allow people to "find" themselves back in the moment with their sensitivity, and ideally only their sensitivity, as their guide. When astrology or divinatory arts go beyond their role, it results in addiction or a mind-game and a corruption of the senses. This is why they were used and known by the very sensitive, who applied them only in times when he/she was disconnected from their intuitive sense. There is no substitute for instinctual sensitivity. These astrological or divinatory methods can help to redirect us back to our senses like a map or guide. To this extent, generality in relation to the whole, when describing someone or a situation, is far more useful than specifics and absolutes. To see Ones-selves within a generality is to start to lose the absolute nature of borders and start to sense unity.

The ancient astrology was an art which was about careful observation of the sky using our faculties of sight and sense.

Now it is electronically programmed into a computer. Various "influences" are evident which, prior to the twentieth century, were not discernable by the human eye. Astrology was originally based on the five visible planets in the sky, but today uses all twelve in the solar system. In addition, many more objects and asteroids are plotted for nuances of the patterns expressed. Astrology has gone from an understanding of energetics and the space around planets to a focus on just the planets themselves, the form of things being absolute. This is not the classical idea of the ancient Greeks, Chinese, Egyptians, or Mayans - those who have the most elaborate understanding of the mappings of the sky. The modern use of high astronomical technology to chart that which is about human senses and what we literally see in the sky, not just about astronomical bodies in space, is something that needs to be reconsidered. Usually readings are too symptomatic and context is not seen. Accuracy of specifics of tendency of a person is superficial compared with understanding the underlying energetic pattern and the detail contextualized. A group of tendencies doesn't tell you anything about the relative strength and weakness of an energetic quality without the whole with which to contextualize it. Yin is nothing other than in comparison with yang. This again shows why, even in the astrological arts which are an attempt to help psychological wellness in patients and help them understand their lives in context - if astrology loses the context itself, then it cannot be helpful. Very commonly the zodiac in Classical Chinese astrology is used purely in the calendrical contextual view and the planetary nuances are not considered at all in the reading, as the detail this adds is not as relevant as the energetic base. As with most things in the modern world which have been taken from the Ancient world, the essence is lost without seeing the context in which it is founded.

It is likely that other forms of ancient astrology such as Hellenistic/ancient Greek astrology would also have been less focused on specifics and more about energetics. This is always the way when we look to find the root from the ancient times. It is as if over the years humans have gone from a broad outlook to an microscopic outlook. This is fine if you can see the broadness within the microcosmic, but until quantum physics breaks through into something totally different, which will be similar to ancient philosophy, we are stuck with seeing the very small as a very small part, not as a holographic representation of the whole which would clarify that there is no such thing as separation. It is interesting that astrology was used to help the agricultural understanding of when to grow crops and to cultivate natural movement in relation to nature and the environment. Today, astrology has become tragically less about this and more about the individual focusing on what "my sign" is. In the past, it was for the benefit of the whole population that their charts were read. Astrology has become more and more focused on the individual and his/her power, not the individual in relation to the whole - the background essence has been removed.

It is important to understand that in ancient times the psychological and physiological were one and the same body-spirit is unified. If we try to separate this off then we see that astrology and the talking therapies are all about the spirit and physical therapies are all about the body. Actually however they are just two ends of the same expression. Spirit therapists will talk to the spirit and through this affect the body, body-orientated therapists will connect to the spirit *through* the body. Both are useful but a) for different patients and b) are expressions of different therapists. The combination of therapist and patient makes for the right communication, if it is a match, so that allowance of change can occur. Overall as explained the spirit therapist needs to be aware that the mind is a powerful entangling quality, for the physical therapist this is less of a problem but they may start to get entwined in believing the body is "the only way" of communicating a message. The yin or the yang are two expressions of the same fundamental base, and this base is more yin which is why the physical therapists have a strong foundational base and associate with the female quality. Of course physical does not preclude energetic nor does energetic discount physical - this is a yinyang dynamic so they are part of a continuum of quality.

Psychology, psychotherapy, counselling, and hypnosis

Interestingly the true meaning of "psychology" is the study of the "spirit" rather than the mind on which it has become now mostly focused. While Spirit and mind seem to be similar, spirit is the root and mind is the branch, it is a function of spirit, and body-spirit is unified. Hence to separate out a study just of the spirit is bound to lead to problems of separation from the body, just as a purely mechanistic body therapy will lose contact with the nature of the person whom they are treating. Oneness means Oneness, so at every level the person seen from here is understood, something that psychology needs to consider and does to an extent. Just as with all the other healing arts, the talking therapies can be fully connected to root medicine or completely separated from it. Differentiation must be made between psychology or the theory - including study and psycho-analysis of the mind's identifications - and psychotherapy. For the most part there are several schools of psychology which are ever-multiplying and which inform and turn into a physio-therapeutic technique, of which a new one is formed almost every year. These are often very much an expression of the originator, rather than a holistic picture. Also all of these ideologies are about using the mind to cure the mind's own identification with itself, which is impossibility. Most forms of theoretically- based psychoanalysis (really a form of psychology rather than psychotherapy), are of the Freudian and Jungian schools - similar philosophic ideas of the time were for example Rudolph Steiner's Anthroposophy. These have all declined in focus due to their often long, drawn-out processes which often keep patients tied to practitioners for years at a time. While these theories are based in cultural heritage, especially of the ancient Greek, Indian and the Chinese, although not necessarily acknowledging the root Classical philosophies being acknowledged, they are also heavily tainted by personal ideologies, interpretations and belief systems of the originators, mixed up with intuitive insights.

Their focus often forms historical studies of a person's mind-identity, it is past-based study of the mind-identity pattern, not really an interest in present moment sense and resolution of mind-identity by seeing through it or simply acknowledging its natural function and leaving it at that, not pandering to analysis. The main problem with these applied systems of analysis is again that the in-the-moment energetic diagnosis root is severed, making it difficult to focus on the process of treatment. If psychotherapy is not based in a theoretical approach of an individual but is intuitively sensed/root-Classical in its approach, acknowledging that the mind-identity process cannot be met head on and analyzed/reasoned-with to effect change, but needs to be contextualized, then this is a very different approach. It is no longer past-based and analytical but present-based and sensory and/or somatic orientated. Focus is not in the minute detail of the past but in the present moment experience of life as a foundation for all other investigations. Use of imagery and ideas is never to be taken lightly in this work. If one does that, mind-identification and confirmation of the separate self can so easily occur, especially if the ideas come from a source that is a personal belief system or personal ideology which often is found in the originators of psychology. This is then simply passed on to the patient. It takes a sensitive practitioner to use imagery and meditative approaches such as found, for example, in some forms of Buddhist meditation, which uses imagery of the mind to dissolve self-image. This is always how deep relaxation works, when a person loses them-"self" and senses reality, they have gone past the imagined self and are at One with life, no longer individuated.

Talking therapy, where a patient talks and the counsellor predominantly listens, provides the platform for a cathartic release of emotions, tensions and thoughts, built up over time inside the patient. Release of these is beneficial and makes for a very important part of treatment. However, curative psychotherapy and hypnotics can be greatly enhanced if one senses which direction the person requires to go, in terms of basic heat and cold. People who are manic, over-expanded, and need firm direction and clarity require a cooling direction - a cool and calm approach, which is stereotypically quite yang-masculine in feel. Then there are others who are deficient, weak, and not confident, who they often need to feel warmth and a compassionate connection, which is stereotypically quite yin-feminine in feel. What usually occurs, however, is that psychological-based "techniques" are employed, such as Cognitive Behavioral Therapy (CBT), neuro-linguistic programming (NLP), or other variations conceived by individuals who again have formulated a theory to train the mind out of patterns, which in itself is a dilemma. To train the mind from within itself is something that is a never-ending spiral. Always when process and use of image is used in primal understanding it is to resolve the idea of separation, which in a sense is to resolve the mind's-identity utterly. Replacing the mind's current identity with another masks the issue. This is often why techniques such as these are quickly cottoned onto by commercial and financial idealists who are looking for peak-performance methods of working and those who mentally "programme" themselves to get in tune with this. This is obviously unnatural. It is important to note that medicine doesn't help people live within the modern society nice and calmly, it actually sensitizes them so they can't think of anything better to do than to leave it. Fundamentally, medicine in its primal root and ancient ways draws to the pre-historic, it draws to the animal, the human-animal which we all are pretending doesn't exist and looks to become a "higher" being, though actually this is an idealism based in fear and separation. The basis of health is to return to instinct so "spiritual paths" that are about finding a "higher point" and pushing forwards to get there are deeply dualistic and often nothing to do with their originator's message, They are not to do with the non-dualism of medical Oneness. The methods of psychology attempt to use thought forms to change other thought forms, reminding one of the Einstein quote that "No problem can be solved from the same level of consciousness that created it", expressing the intrinsic issue that blocks curative effect with this modality.

This is not to say that some degree of symptomatic relief isn't possible using techniques of changing thought patterns towards "the positive" rather than "the negative" but it doesn't deal with the underlying fact that this is still a dualism being compounded. Going beyond the thought form or emotion is always the way that a curative process of treatment can be found. This may be well-known by practitioners of various forms of psychotherapy, who simply use these structures as formats for treating and within this they work intuitively. Any applied ideology is nothing when compared to practitioners with sensitivity and diagnostic ability in the present moment.

That said, there are numerous practitioners who constantly go beyond the boundaries of their therapy because they intuitively sense that the connection requires another approach. There are many therapeutic styles in the modern arena, some are cooler and some warmer, depending on the originator of the practice. Gestalt therapy and ideologies such as Werner Erhard's who created "the Forum" and "Landmark", are cold, clear and direct, while Ericksonian hypnosis, for example, helps the mind to let go through more yin, warmer and less direct understanding. Interestingly both ideologies are about drawing the attention to being present rather than getting involved in past mind-based unravelling, which actually compounds the problems. Very often, it is not the words the practitioners say which matter most, but how they are said. This is why hypnosis, when used with a psychotherapeutic approach not informed by theoretical-psychological ideas, comes closest to the Shamanistic direction used by all the ancient cultures. If linked to primal medicine, practitioners of this kind often get to the root of the mind-identified pattern and problem much faster and more directly than another practitioner would with a purely physical approach.

These days, the mental and physical bodies are seen as separate, the body sense and the mind expression can be almost entirely opposite for someone and this may be considered "normal." This often requires a mind-direct application, rather than only through the body, indirectly affecting the mental-emotional patterns, in order to allow the patient to relax. A combined mental and physical treatment is often the most effective, but some practitioners lean towards the mental-spiritual (yang) arts, and some towards the physical-energetic (yin) arts. Some, who are in the middle, are both. This generally depends on the nature of the practitioner him/herself, or "tool" they use.

Above are but a few of the therapies derived from the ancient ways, but which are following narrower structures due to the nature of our times. The key is to acknowledge the root principles of yinyang (or similar) in all these expressions of treatment. This allows what is limited to be able to connect and form a whole. One doesn't need to do all therapies or have all the tools, in fact, some say it is best to be very good at one expression than to know many tools and spread oneself too thinly. I feel that whether you use a few or many tools, the key is in the connection to the patients and the knowing of your own expression as a person, as to whether you are a person who likes a lot of tools or just a few, but always in context and with sense of the whole spectrum and one's place within it. This is simply understanding root-theory and allowing it to be a mirror to see clearly and to draw one back when the mental-separation starts to take over. If you can't help, or find the outer border of an expression, someone else may be able to, but the background diagnostic sense will remain the same for all involved. The process becomes impersonal and yet deeply intimate. A paradox of nature.

The whole notion and direction of this book is to see that although individuals and even cultures have their own style of expression, what brings this into context is the universal energetic understanding and "language". This can allow us to see beyond the borders of what we are individually, and to see and practise medicine conscious of its unified holism. In this way we can appreciate that it is "taught" or sensed and practised and theorized. The closer the medical format is to being able to express itself in the context of energetic, not restricted by modern Newtonian idealism (see below discussion) this will allow a seamless unity to be felt. For example the root Classical medicines of Chinese and Ayurveda are seamless in their unity at a base level and this is conscious. Of course the practitioner and his/her individual effectiveness are not being assessed here, as healing is always an energetic occurrence at root which is not about the individual, despite the idea of the individual. This means becoming aware of this fact, rather than fighting against it or attempting to stay within mental constraints and not seeing the very ancient, and yet very alive immediate realization of the energetic root of all healings. A style or method of practice is a model, a mental idea we adopt. If it is one of the many styles above, it will be of a specific individual's mind. If this model is too narrow in any way, it will mean that we take on this narrowness ourselves and it shapes our minds, rather than frees them.

The approach of what is said above and the acknowledgement of the Classical root of medicine (written by no individual), is to set free the mind and the senses and allow medicine to be practised and understood totally intuitively. Also we notice that, in the end, the intuitions of different expressions meet in the middle or Centre, so to speak, so it is best then to not alienate each other's differences, but to see the unity that binds us together as a single hand with numerous fingers of expression. If we consider that primal medicine has a single tool with a billion different heads - from the fine to the medium to the coarse - then "New Age" medicine is like a smaller group of medium and fine-headed tools which are focused on intently and begin to separate from one another. Modern medicines are the heaviest, coarsest tools, and also separate from one another - all there is are these tools to the exclusion of everything else, whereas the primal root healing therapies use whatever is appropriate. The "New Age" ones are limited, but due to theoretical constraints impede the healing process. The modern medicines are even more limited and more impeded. In modern treatment, a lot of force is generally used, it's like a theoretical armoured jacket. In "New Age" treatments medium and light force is used to go past the resistance of the theory; in ancient medicine treatments everything is appropriate and without force. This grading is a result of fragmentation from the root. The further one goes and the more one separates itself from the core, the less balance one has and the easier it is to break. Individual leaves and smaller branches break all the time, and large branches break off occasionally, but even if the trunk breaks, the roots generally remain untouched and can spring new growth. The upper branches are always at risk: they can be easily broken, are more exposed and the newest, the most energetically "expensive" and beautiful, full of bright leaves; if they are not in contact with the root of their energy and are "going it alone," they will soon wither and die. Even if the root is hidden from view, it is always present behind the picture.

In nature, the higher you go, the lighter and more open life has to become. The upper branches are then one with the root, reliant on it for nutrients. However, as we go up the medical tree, as we see it today, we find the heaviest, most rigid structures at the top. The tree is, in fact, top-heavy, just like the human mind-identification process; our egos are worn like a crown on a single leaf. It's likely to use up its quota of energy and fall over, like a rootless tree. So we now ascend into the upper branches of medicine. We will have a look at these most separated and most individuated of structures and notice how they compare to the rest of the modalities. Again, this is not a criticism of the modern style, it is an effort to contextualize the whole picture, so we know what's what and so we can see the root and background differentiated from the branches and foreground. When something that aims to contextualize sounds like a critical process this is something that the practitioner must look within themselves to understand. It is possible you might feel that I have not fully recognized your theoretical position in whatever field you trained, but I'm really looking to find the therapist within you who is not attached to a particular genre and is what you are behind confinement, for here is where there is unity a situation without labels, an expression without name, a map without borders.

3. Modern fragmented medicine naturopathy (and vitamin, mineral, and trace element supplementation)

Naturopathy is a form of medicine that has been around for about one-hundred and sixty years; Vincent Priessnitz (1799-1851) who was a farmer, is credited as the "Father of Naturopathy". It is based today almost wholly in modern bio-medicine, so Newtonian science is still its mainstay. However, naturopathic practitioners focus on naturally-found biochemical structures from herbs and foods that can be curative, and only then draw them out bio-chemically into a fragmented particle, like a vitamin. Diagnostics are based on Western medical ideology and as such focus on the symptoms of a problem. For example, with a case of high blood pressure, one would focus on the heart and the vascular system as the cause of the problem. With viral infections and bacterial infections, one would attempt to clear out the pathological viruses and bacteria and find products which naturally "boost the immune system." Naturopathy is very popular because it has the so-called advantage of being scientific, while still using "natural" ideas within treatment.

For example, Patrick Holford is a key proponent of supplementation. Naturopaths very often prescribe a lot of vitamins and mineral supplements, as well as trace elements which act like catalysts in the body. The basic premise of the whole process is tonification and provision of what the body needs, which is a very allopathic concept and is in a sense its primary connection to root medicine. However, the ancient principle of

119

finding what the body needs, which is to get the person back to their natural instincts, is compromised by focusing on the machinery of diagnostics more than with the patient, and placing focus on getting a blood test and analyzing it, charting stool consistency and blood pressure, and numerous activities which, interestingly, family GP's (General (bio-medical) practitioner) of the past used to do. Some naturopaths may palpate patients and do physical diagnostics as well. These practitioners focus on finding mineral and vitamin deficiencies and either change dietary regimes to suit this (although they may send these people to a dietician or nutritionist), or more often will find the right supplement to suit the patient. In recent years, homeopathy has started to encroach into this field, which is inconsistent from the foundational principles view, as the general allopathic-focused prescriptions are contra-indicative to homeopathic direction.

Getting two different directions of treatment at the same time - cathartic and tonic - is like listening to two conversations at once or eating a starter and dessert at the same time. One can perform local catharsis to an area of the body, but in a background of allopathic, or one can go all-out and do all catharsis. But to do a bit of allopathy and a bit of homeopathy on a systemic level is totally counter-productive and confusing to the body-spirit. The key problem with naturopathy is the supplementation of the various forms of fragmented medicines like vitamins and minerals and trace elements. The idea that these are "natural" supplements is sometimes not true, as they can be synthetically created, although naturally-created ones are often recommended. The other problem is that there are always new scientific discoveries about the fragments of vitamins and minerals: one day, tea will be very bad for you, the next very good; the same for red wine, coffee, and chocolate. You have heard this all before, and this is because they are still caught in the dualism of "good-for-you-bad-for-you" type ideology. It can never be "right" because every patient is different, and so there is never a "right" approach. The process of ingesting these vitamins and minerals is also very difficult for the body, as it cannot identify these supplements as a food, since food doesn't behave in the way these things do. They are more similar to a refined substance like sugar or salt, high concentrations of biochemicals that flood the blood and body with much more than it can handle. As a result, they pass out in the urine in a wasteful way, being driven through the liver and kidneys, over-working and eventually weakening them, creating the "rainbow" coloured urine effect, so common in the modern age.

Trace elements are considered to have catalyzing qualities of helping the body's process of change towards healing, but in the same way as all forms of supplementation with a non-energetic diagnostic understanding, the use of medicines is deeply limited and as such they can be used inappropriately to the primal diagnostic language as mentioned before. The difficulty is that humans are not fragmented creatures and so fragmented foods cause problems. They make people continue to be fragmented in their body-spirit. This effect is spread all the way through the system, for wholeness needs to ingest wholeness in the foods one eats. This is basic, even before whatever quality the food is and whether you can taste the difference between chemically-created food and organic food, which, for most, is obvious. We have to start with holism. This is basically a form of bio-medicine without the pharmaceutical drugs - in place of the pharmaceutical industry we have the supplement and vitamin industry. Of the therapies, is not particularly subtle in its approach. This kind of medicine however , as we will see with all modern medicines, fits well with the modern lifestyle, that of being able to fly from one side of the whole to another, having some lunch and then coming back again, or taking a person from their native environment and placing them in another which is totally different and impossible to adapt to within a single generation.

Such situations and modern ways of thinking and fragmenting the world-view bring within it a requirement to keep the system stable. This means that those who become deeply dependent on these nutritional supports generally are maladapted to the situation and climate and every conceivable nuance in between. This is impossible to supplement but sometimes supplements can act as a crutch here. As we explained before, primal medicine is that which takes one back to instinct and to the place of origin: what we eat, what climate is suitable and what is right for us. Even in this world of anti-indigenous and anti-native we still have these seeds within us and the instinct to go towards what suits us best. No form of medicine which holds the status quo will cure, as it contains problem; also it will use many resources in attempting to do so.

Nutrition therapy, dietetics, and western herbal medicine

These subjects are akin to naturopathy but are in the realm of a less "medical" approach because they are concerned with food, rather than medicinal supplementation. The nutritionists are scientifically-trained and based in the constantly changing pinpoint focus of the bio-medical world, which finds different specifics about different food all the time. Often, naturopaths will learn nutritional theories and so will incorporate foods and supplementation together into their practice, or they may work together with a separate nutritionist. Nutrition involves studying food and creating diets for individuals, based on bio-medical analysis and diagnosis. It is also concerned with theoretical regimes of the various styles of individual researchers who teach nutrition. Dr. Lawrence Plaskett, for example, focused on teaching about the sodium /potassium balance of the blood, with a direction towards potassium intake in food being more beneficial than sodium, as generally everyone's diet has too much sodium in it. Of course, this is similar to yinyang: sodium could be considered more yang (or acidic) than potassium (more alkaline/yin), relative to each other, although is looking from within a fragmented model. As a result, Dr. Plaskett's diets were cooling and so the people who could benefit were those who were too heated. Generally most people in the west and the tendency for most humans is to over-heat (especially men) rather than to over-cool, however this does not account for the whole and as a result large groups will not be clearly considered. Women have far less over-heating capacity, especially during menstrual years, so this broader view is often not often considered. The cooler patients would not do well on his diet. So again, there is limitation here, due both to a theoretical approach and a bio-chemical means of understanding, rather than the Oneness of energetics.

Dr. Gerson, inventor of the Gerson therapy which is often used in cancer treatment, has a similar but more aggressive tack. Other nutrition-based theorists like Dr. Peter J. D'Adamo, who was the inventor of the blood-type diet, and numerous other dietary gurus, are now providing diets which attempt to find a trace of a person's ancestry, in order to understand their dietary requirements. Brilliant and surprising as this move is, which is a distinct understanding of our ancient heritage of Oneness with the earth, the bio-chemical ideology behind these diets makes them quite restrictive and fragmentary, and D'Adamo's original idea, which comes close to energetically investigating the body constitution, is stopped by a process of dietary analysis at the chemical level. This cuts off the understanding of unity and so can end up confusing.

Western herbal medicine is really an extension of nutritional therapy in that it now bio-chemically analyses the properties of herbs and prescribes based on an understanding of the bio-chemistry of the patient through signs, symptoms, blood analysis, urine analysis, and more. Some Western herbalists will focus on the energetics, which then allows them to be wholly connected to ancient medicine, in the same way that *Culpeper's Herbal* is a foundation for this kind of folk medicine in Western herbal literature. However, this is becoming rarer, due to the might of Western bio-medicine, which is now taking over herbs in the same fragmentary way as the ideology behind supplementation and food. The problem with nutritional therapy is that it looks at whole foods in a fragmented way, thereby creating a lack of deep connection with the food and seeing it as a means to an end, focusing on its calories and quantities rather than its energetics. For both acute and chronic issues, dieticians prescribe serious dietary changes in a Western medical setting for weight loss and nutritional control. Dieticians are more part of bio-medicine and modern Western medicine, they are often in hospitals and are directly referred to by doctors.

Chiropractic medicine

Chiropractic was founded in 1895 by Daniel David Palmer. Palmer's vision at this time was one of an understanding of medicine which was close to energetic understanding of "vitalism" and unified understanding of the body and universe. At this time Chiropractic medicine would have been associated very much with a connection to the bone-setting aspects of An-massage, for example within the Classical Chinese approach, or have connection to the massage and healing techniques of ancient Greece. However as time when on Chiropractic medicine became more and more mainstream-associated and focused in materialistic concepts. Originally Chiropractic medicine would have been seen within the "New age" group above but today there is a heavy alignment with Western medical applications, sometimes crossing over into other categories of treatment, not just the bones and nerves but all mostly with an outlook which is materialist. Chiropractors most often take this view and as such have gained referral and more interest by western bio-medicine and GP's who may refer to them because of the similarity in understanding. Often chiropractors today will use X-ray images to assess bone and nerve-associated problems. Machinery such as spinal traction and spring-loaded devices called activators which create small amounts of thrust to make spinal and other "corrections" have become very commonly used in chiropractic clinics.

Chiropractors are interested mainly in bones and nerves and their various interactions. The spine is their key point of interaction and they focus on "putting right" areas of held tension, commonly, although not always, through forceful means to push bones back to where they "should" be. The problem with this type of approach, as with so many others, is that the focus is very narrow so other structures like the muscles and tendons are less focused on. As such, manipulations can be done without considering the patient as an overall whole. So if tension is due to an overall cold pattern, chiropractic medicine can worsen the problem and even be dangerous to the patient. If there is high tension in the upper body, with heat patterns, then the patient can handle the manipulation and bone adjustments. However, because the soft tissues around the region are far less considered than the bone-nerve tissue, spasms and nerve reactions can happen as well which can be dangerous, especially around the neck. Here, the "problem," or narrow viewpoint, restricts the practices and this is when the practitioner is not using his or her senses, instead allowing a mechanical approach to take over. In fact this is the key problem also with all materialist viewpoints and the whole modern thought process; and so with medicine, it is further and further allowing the sensitivities of the practitioner to be taken over by increasingly expensive equipment, rather than using sense and the age-old perfect expression of the human body to do the sensing. The idea of using machines is a very, very coarse ideology. The human is in fact so subtle and sensitive that machines cannot keep up in efficiency and unparallelled performance. The belief in the machine is the belief in mind-identity, the tool of the mind, over the human sense itself. This is a form of madness.

As such, chiropractic medicine can rarely see the root of the problem. The main areas of root are regions of deficiency, slackness, looseness and weakness, rather than areas of tightness and blocking. Chiropractic medicine, as with all modern medicine, looks at the physicality of pain and symptoms, not the root deficiency and suffering. Therefore, it is always focused on areas of excess and on localities, rather than on generalities and systemic functions. As a result, one constantly needs a chiropractor to click the back into shape again, something which can keep the patient reliant unless the practitioner goes beyond the approach and sees the whole. It is very uncommon for a therapeutic style to go from being a "modern method" theory to becoming a "new age" method, i.e. expansion; it is much more common for what we see in chiropractic medicine and osteopathy, even acupuncture and similar disciplines, to be drawn into the "rationalism" of modern medicine which is a belief system in itself of pure materialism/ separatism. The mind of the humans is much more likely to focus in and be distracted on detail than it is to open outwards and expand. The primal medicine of the ancients comes from the expanded plain which is why all these therapies roots are deeply involved in the whole picture, but the modern mentality is unable to see this.

Osteopathy

Originally osteopathy and chiropractic medicine were part of the same group, then chiropractic splintering away due to its own focuses and theories. Although there is much more to it in the sense of theory and subtlety, osteopathy is a generally a gentler and more rounded expression compared to chiropractic medicine from the context of the original bone-setting base tradition from which both therapies originate in the ancient understanding. It considers more of the body but still has no fundamental energetic basis, although it swings towards a sense of it and realizes interconnectedness of the body as vital. However it is stuck very much with Western medical organ systems and understands pathology and physiology in these terms. Osteopathy, as a treatment, works on the soft tissues to ease the process of making "corrections" of the spine and other regions of the body. It considers the body much more as a musculo-skeletal system, rather than skeletal-neurological, as in the modern chiropractor's approach. It contains everything that chiropractors do and is fast becoming a doctor's preferred referral tool over chiropractors and even physiotherapists.

Osteopathy, however, still has a fundamental problem in that it isn't energetic-based. In ancient medicine, for example Chinese medicine, osteopathy would be part of the bone-setting procedures of An-massage, which is classical massage and healing of the meridians. Because diagnosis has a fundamental basis in yinyang, one would very easily be able to know if the patient can take manipulation today, or if a different treatment is needed before manipulation can be undertaken. A cold patient should not be manipulated and this is not recognized by osteopathic ideas. Andrew Taylor Still (1828 - 1917) founded osteopathy and was a mechanist in numerous ways, although he recognised that the body was unified and wanted to look for an approach that was not mainstream medicine, but it was only when William Sutherland started to reform osteopathy, including energetic ideology that created cranio-sacral osteopathy, that there was a further move towards the energetic medicine. As has happened so often with naturopathy, chiropractic medicine, osteopathy and many others inevitably to be seen as "okay" by the western medical fraternity, this means to sell one's soul towards a bio-medical outlook which in turn takes out the energetics that were being sniffed out by the originators. If one had taken the different course of going with these original insights then theoristic stylism would vanish to re-unite with the background unity of medicinal Oneness.

Colonic irrigation

Enemas have been used for years as part of purgative treatment in order to clear heat and toxicity (which are both the same, in Oriental medicine) from the body. Colonics, therefore, is nothing new, it is just more advanced in its technology. This would originally have been part of ancient herbal healing, incorporating enemas and herbal enemas, which have particular effects on the bowels, almost always cooling. The procedure is very useful for fevers and for high temperature. It can have a lowering effect on blood pressure and high tension in the system, and as with the water, heat can be cleared out. It is useful for heat but not for cold.

Bio-resonance therapy and allergy testing methods

The essential idea of bio-resonance therapy is to locate stuck energy and regions of the body which are in pain or malaise in some form. Everything has a resonance, so the goal is to find the resonating electro-magnetic frequency of the region of the pain or problem and then to play back the opposite resonant frequency by use of a computer, to counteract it. Since the human being has a resonance, foods and allergens that affect the resonant frequency of the human in a healthy state can be identified and avoided. This is also the principle of many allergy-testing equipments, although variations on how this is done and the ideas behind it are numerous. Again, this is not new. Waves are energy. All diagnosis is seeing distortions in the energy field, either sensing them or touching them. With these methods the machine is taking over the individual's sense, making it lazier and redundant.

Bio-resonance attempts to bring modern physics into the biological arena. Many such tools are being investigated, including those used for diagnostics and imaging, such as MRI and CAT scans. These tools may be different in many ways, but they are all bulky extensions of the senses we have. An over-reliance on these results in a loss of our own sensitivity. All modern forms of diagnosis lack energetic context, so it is vital to use them to their best possible advantage, sparingly and in acute situations. Bio-resonance is highly scientific and therefore those using it can refuse to see anything but that approach, except those individual practitioners who wish to broaden outwards. These practitioners step into the energetic world, to which other Western medically-tooled therapists are more resistant. This is as close as Newtonian physics gets towards a biological connection and field theory of the biological being, which is associated with biologists like Rupert Sheldrake in his morphogenic field theory.

Considerably more than just a set of wave patterns is understood through touch. Many of the greatest medical intuitive practitioners of the Chinese expression need only to take the pulse once, and then they can tell the whole person's medical history. This is not just because of the various forms and nuances of the pulse, the touch is a connection of the two energetic beings, so memories and senses are shared, so to speak. This may sound too much like Star Trek, but if we really consider our sensitivity as being a prime investigator in the world and we understand that bats can locate themselves in the total darkness while flying, our touch is not such an acute sense. Bio-resonance allies itself to acupuncture because the practitioners use the acupuncture points as seats of electromagnetic charge from the modern perspective. Qi/ ki/ spirit or prana (depending on the same meaning of a word being used all over the ancient world) is all of energy, not one kind split off from the others which makes it "scientific." To truly experience natural medicine, one needs to take a step into the background picture and not be too focused on the tools.

Allergy testing, of any kind, is hampered by the problem of what patients are allergic to *now*, not what the problem is that is causing the allergy. Instead of finding the root with this therapy, one restricts the diet. It is a way of dealing with it and often true intolerances or toxins, which are impossible to digest, can be removed from the diet - but then again, people eat aeroplanes! (e.g. Michel Lotito of France; Guinness world record holder for "Strangest diet" eats 900g of metal per day!) Why is it that some people can eat aeroplanes and others cannot? It has to do with constitution and the strength of the energy. If "immunity" is increased - meaning if energy in the body is increased due to a more sensitive feel of the world and a more healthy body - then allergies fade and go away. The whole physiological system can change. Again, allergy testing focuses on the symptoms, not the root. The body knows how to choose food and instinctively knows how to heal and clear out pathogens and toxins, so if this mechanism is made more efficient, if this sensitivity is enhanced, then the body can go to a state of peace. Although it is important that people sense their food and move towards an ancestrallybased diet associated with their energetic constitution, allergy testing can be a way of initiating this process by suggesting foods that really get in the way and are obviously destructive to the system. The problem is that there is no context for what is deeply right for the patient or an understanding of their constitution and what kinds of energy works with it, just foods that at a specific time are "good for you" or "bad for you". This is dualistic and so leads to this same process of the patient's interaction to food as to the world, it doesn't necessarily direct to unity and sense within their bodies, which is really the art of healing.

Physiotherapy

Physiotherapy is a form of treatment that is now very popular in modern medicine. It is basically a form of rehabilitation and a support system for those who have suffered accidents and injuries, but is also used with the elderly and disabled, ante/post natal well-being, relaxation and body awareness for mental health patients and further numerous applications in physical health care. For patients who are unable to move themselves or require passive movement to keep circulation going, physiotherapy works to re-stimulate nerves and keeps the body moving and operating. Physiotherapy focuses on the limb movements, mobility, breathing, general physical movement, and kinesthetics. It is really an extension of the traditional role of nursing. Physiotherapists motivate patients and help them to regain movement after operations, sometimes also treating the body with massage, dry needling, or trigger-point acupuncture to help release tense tissues. [Note: The idea behind this and what is termed "medical acupuncture" often done by both doctors and physiotherapists after a 2 - 3 week course, is to treat locally, using needles and stimulating nerves. The direction is entirely different from energetic medicine, so this can't be seen as the use of acupuncture as a part of the ancient understanding.

Sometimes electro-acupuncture, or the use of TENS-machines which provide electrical stimulation to muscles, are also part of this type of work.]

Physiotherapy is less focused than other forms of treatment. It does try to see the whole person in the environment they live in, and physiotherapists are often involved with other practitioners, like occupational therapists, who try to change the patient's physical environment or adapt tools to suit his/her needs. Physiotherapists offer posture and exercise routines that help train the body back to a level of health, so that the patient does not require treatment any more. The physiotherapist makes his/her own diagnosis, but it is usually based on a doctor's analysis of the patient's condition. The physiotherapist's diagnosis is more practically-orientated towards mobility and keeping everything moving - for example, gradually increasing the movement in the limbs, helping to ease the patient's pain. Although the approach still sees the body as a set of blocks of muscle, bone and tissue and doesn't see energy, making the treatments rather coarse or mechanical if followed rigidly as this is the theoretical base, it is very much patient-centred, most physiotherapists are caring and focused on patients, making them one of the few healing therapists of modern medicine. This said however, the whole ideology of a non-energetic basis for treatment means that they can be unaware of the obvious and can therefore over-massage cold patients and under-massage hot patients. This can lead to using too much force to open up tense joints and end up causing more damage.

Also the bureaucratic-legal process which is an attempt to prevent legal action of the patient or family of the patient has increasingly hampered all forms of medicine but very heavily associated with the modern aspects. This has meant massive cut-back in actual engagement of the practitioner with the patient so there is a fear around this process. This is common now to many medically-based practices, something which is the ultimate expression of separation and economic idealism, and utterly opposite to medicine. However sometimes the intuitive nature of the therapist involved overrides the theoretical rigidity and bureaucratic prison of the purely mechanistic view. Physiotherapists might use additional treatments, like acupuncture, do osteopathic training or add other approaches like aromatherapy and massage, although again the root principle of these therapies is often overlooked. Still, they are an inlet valve of possible new ideas into the Western medical arena and, as are nurses, they are the caring aspect of the health care system. This caring aspect can support health, despite its ideology, because of its humanness and connection.

Psychiatry

A psychiatrist is a doctor who specializes in the bio-medical treatment of patients with mental illness. Treatment often involves bio-medical drugs and sometimes institutionalization in very bad cases. These doctors consider the brain as a purely biochemical system which can be manipulated with additional introduced chemicals in order to make behavioural changes. This process should be used only for acute situations, considering the "sledge-hammer" effect of the power of the drugs that they wield. Unfortunately, psychiatrists often prescribe for chronically ill patients and this often deepens the patients' problems in terms of side-effects and further mental health issues. With an approach as fragmented as this with the brain, the head, the focus and bio-medicine as the methodology, it is very difficult to see how people can actually be healed or cured by this form of treatment. Rather, they are prevented from being a "problem" to people around them. These patients' problems are often controllable, although not in the prescribed way. The highly barbaric treatments of electric shock and surgical removal of aspects of the brain took place until only forty years ago. Psychiatry is a new medicine and is strongly powered by the pharmaceutical industry.

Modern western biomedicine

To be more easily understood, modern medicine can be split into three main tools of treatment: bio-medicinal drugs, surgery, and nursing. These treatments are based on a highly focused diagnosis of what in ancient medicine would be called symptoms *only*. This means that very often from a foundational breadth of view, diagnosis and treatment is as the "leaves and branches" of a person, focusing on the superficial symptomatic issues. It is not at all interested, or worse not acknowledging the existence of the whole rest of the "tree" that is the live human being in the dis-ease of suffering. The physical condition can be seen and dealt with, but the energetic is a total mystery, even though it underpins everything that goes on in the process of healing. Bowel cancer, brain tumour, physical injury are all seen and focused on, but the patterns that originated these illnesses at the deepest level of the energetic, are not. Diagnostics in biomedicine are now almost entirely focused on a machine's analysis, whether it be of blood, urine, stool, tissues in an MRI, CAT scans and bones in X-rays, or soft tissue by ultra-sound. The number of diagnostic tools increases each year, and the technology for treatment, drugs and surgery is constantly developing. The use of bio-medicinal drugs is a tunnel-vision of the tree of ancient herbal medicine. Physical therapeutics has been handed over to the physiotherapists, and the body is seen from only a highly mechanical perspective where healing touch is of no significance.

Surgery, (and its subsidiary dentistry), is the hero of the modern Western clinic's power. It is a highly advanced and focused activity requiring exceptional skill and using high technology, usually of military origin. Nursing, however, is still a healing art form. We find numerous situations where the nurse not only knows more than the doctor as far as procedures are concerned, because they have more experience, but they also play the role of the true healer - which is one of provision of care and compassion and connection. Women primarily do this job and always have done. When their healing is taken out of the picture there is a great essential quality that is missing from medicine. Nurses interact with patients and help in seemingly small ways, affecting the atmosphere and overall environment, as well as offering the specific care. This engenders a background consciousness and a sense of seeing the wood for the trees. Of course, this is becoming less and less the case, as bureaucracy is devouring this profession. Yet, the greater connection to healing and health lies with the nurses, rather than the doctors. From Florence Nightingale:

> *"Pathology teaches the harm that disease has done. But it teaches nothing more. We know nothing of the principle of health, the positive of which pathology is the negative, except from observation and experience. And nothing but observation and experience will teach us the ways to maintain or to bring back the state of health. It is often thought that medicine is the curative process. It is no such thing. Medicine is the surgery of functions, as surgery proper is that of limbs and organs. Neither can do anything but remove obstructions, neither can cure; nature alone cures. Surgery removes the bullet out of the limb, which is an obstruction to cure, but nature heals the wound. So it is with medicine, the function of an organ becomes obstructed - medicine, so far as we know, assists nature to remove the obstruction, but does nothing more."* (Nightingale, 1859).

Surgery is a true art but is not medicine in the same sense. It is about dexterity and artistry and connection to a complex structure. Being a surgeon is more like being an artist, a carpenter, or watch-maker, because it is possible for a surgical procedure to go very well and yet for the patient to die. This is because it is not only about physiology, but about cutting, fixing and reshaping; it's a dead subject with live material to work on - and a vital one. The anaesthetist is the most holistic practitioner on the surgical team, monitoring the whole patient the whole time, like a background, so that the surgeon can do his work. Surgery is a highly skilful field, which shows ingenuity and inventive technology. However, it is about fragmentation, about splitting things apart and putting things together in parts; therefore it is always about separation - what we do best within the mind-identified state of Newtonian materialism. Medicine of this kind is war against the exterior. It attempts to keep the parts of the body together in one piece and yet to keep the organism separate from the world, with aggressive "protection" meaning hygienic aggression (anti-biotics), against the environment and so also in fact the human as he/she is part of nature. It's a vicious circle of nature fighting itself, an auto-immune dis-ease in its own right, which is the nature of the modern human's effect on him/herself and the environment.

General practitioners (GPs) look at patients with the help of the various tools at their disposal, such as scanners and blood tests. Contact with the actual patient is hardly necessary, as they can refer the patient on to whichever specialist is appropriate. This specialization ideology, which is a result of the fragmentation of medicine and not looking at the whole, applies to all of medicine. Soon there will be an ear doctor, nose doctor, and throat doctor, all in different rooms. The whole body will be mapped out into different, ever-increasing fragments. A lack of communication results, as does any connection to the unity they are in fact parts of, just like numerous other medicines we have looked at in this "upper branch/leaf-focused" category. The modern medical model is based on modern mind-identity, it is one of total fragmentary thinking, with everything isolated and everything identified. This medicine is fragile, reliant on huge supplies of power and huge networks of energy, it is inefficient and often unable to unify, because no specialist will understand the language the others speak.

In fact all dis-ease is auto-immune in this sense, all dis-ease is the nature of the human mind attacking itself, this means sufferance. It is based on the underlying premise that we "have to survive" and that Herbert Spencer was correct with regard to "survival of the fittest." The problem with Spencer's idea, as applied to Charles Darwin's evolutionary science, is that it is not looking at the whole picture. The whole idea of evolution is obviously true, but the premise that it is about survival is a purely human connotation based upon our primal fear of death. No other animal has this fear, they just respond to what is there. So, you might say, why would a zebra run when a lion is chasing it? What would be the point? Why doesn't it just bow its head and allow itself to be eaten? This too is all about yinyang. The yang expression of the expansional energy of the zebra means that it wants to expand and grow; the lion also wants to expand and grow. The energy of the lion is direct and its power pushes it like a magnet on the zebra, who responds by running in the opposite direction. The zebra cannot be what it is with the lion's presence, so it moves somewhere where it can open and expand. If the lion is stronger the zebra will not be able to do this, and so the zebra gives way to the lion's energy which strengthens the lion-energy field. If the zebra gets away, then it is like the transformation at this time does not occur, the energy field is in balance of lion and zebra-field. The two, of course, are not separate, but they seem to be and language perpetuates this idea. It is not true that this is about survival. It is about life, living, polarity, energetics. Survival is about the fear of death. The lion and zebra do not think about death, they are always free of the ideas of life and death, living on the knife-edge of existence. Why should we apply our logic to them, or indeed to ourselves, when it is wholly unnatural?

It is actually the case that most modern biologists do not use the phrase "survival of the fittest," and it was not a term that Darwin originated. Herbert Spencer first used the phrase, after reading Charles Darwin's "*On the Origin of Species*", in his *Principles of Biology* (1864), in which he drew parallels between his own economic theories and Darwin's biological ones. He wrote: "This survival of the fittest, which I have here sought to express in mechanical terms, is that which Mr. Darwin has called 'natural selection,' or the preservation of favoured races in the struggle for life." (quoted in the re-published text: Spencer H., 2009). This being the case, it is interesting that medicine still pertains to and focuses on an economic "struggle"; medicine seems confined to this narrow image of reality. This whole notion blocks medicine and is completely eradicated by science, even with its Newtonian dualism, particularly by physics. Physics holds the key to non-judgmental ideas and understanding non-survivalist mentality, or evolution without judgment. Subtly, within modern medicine, is the idea that death is bad and life (surviving) is good, and herein lies the very basis upon which medicine stands apart from science. It is indeed a form of moralizing, rather than being the pure objectivity that medicine is believed to be. True objectivity would require us to lose our focus on survival and instead focus on the quality of health (meaning "wholeness") or allowing the lessening of sufferance (meaning "separatism"). This is at the heart of what corrupts modern medicine and makes it a very religious institution.

Biology too is manipulated and directed by medicine, as are bio-chemistry and most of physics, for the "greater good of humanity." All of this is the same moralizing, and still at some point involves a religious figure taking over from the doctor, when "no more can be done". The physicians are not scientific, and far from being outside of religious dogma they require dualistic religion. However, the outer reaches of modern physics seem incorruptible by anything other than the need to know and gain clarity about the nature of the universe. These are the particle and cosmological physicists, the only ones who have no direction for their studies other than to find the truth. Science, other than this, is all "intended"; there is no discovery any more, only intended results and outcomes - as opposed to true inquest into absolute mystery. Darwin used the term "natural selection" to describe a process that was happening for no known reason, an unknowable ideology. Darwin was ,through his own limitations as a modern thinker, a true naturalist, someone who was interested the way of nature. This, too, is the ancient way. Nature knows why one animal continues its line and the other doesn't; the human cannot in a sense "know", unless from a broader plain that is not about analysis but about intuitive sense. This too brings in a spiritual rather than religious, or perhaps existential quality, but one of wonder and not knowing, rather than one of absolutes and power struggles. This ideology doesn't come from fear.

Science, in its true form, is also derived from this wonder, and if only the science - in this true or "Pure" sense - started to complete itself by looking back at the observer of the experiment, then the observer would find the root to all their queries and perceptions, the very background from where they originate. Unfortunately, it is not this true sense of inquiry that science harnesses, but rather big business and big industry. This too is the plight of medicine and the economic ideology of "survival of the fittest." It is a far cry from the Hippocratic ancestry in ancient Greek medicine. There is an imbalance in Western medicine: it is hierarchical and it is, as a result, fragile, but it cannot see this. It is top-heavy medicine, its branches full of the heaviest tools imaginable, and it can easily break and fall, but with the root and the unity of energetic understanding constantly present at the base and background, waiting. It is a root-less realm, where a patient can be treated like a number or a name, not an expression of the whole. The doctor him/herself very often quickly forgets the original reason for practising medicine and becomes overloaded by bureaucratic rules and regulations and the pharmaceutical industry pushing new drug inventions to try out. The biochemical drug industry is renowned for being focused on profit making, not healing, it no longer has the credibility to be considered part of medical expression, but is more about economics. Many of the pharmaceutical drugs that are of any value are for use in acute situations and only work to remove symptoms, as they come from this mindset. There are exceptions to this, of course. Pharmaceutical drugs will normally cause dependence over a long period of use. They are non-curative from the perspective of ancient medicine as the suffering is not the focus but rather the pain or symptom, and therefore one doesn't expect relief from symptoms unless one keeps taking them. Isn't there something wrong with this? The key is to engage with the root, but if you don't understand, or feel it is an archaic or "unproven" way of considering life, you have to keep taking the medicines.

Modern Western bio-medicine, within the spectrum of those therapies we have looked at, has a very narrow bandwidth of use. It is best for the acute physical problems, such as for acute physical injury or acute physical illnesses. Here, emergency medicine, which requires surgery and/or very cooling medication like antibiotics, is where Western medicine can help. It helps with the symptoms and removes the problem in a physical and aggressive way. For all chronic and non-acute illnesses, however, there is absolutely no requirement for modern medicine, except for those already caught in the drug loop. These people would be better off weaning themselves off the drugs to get to health. Those connected to machines such as dialysis are connected to this process for life. Already the illness is too physical and has damaged the body, so this kind of constant acute situation requires this kind of intervention. However, those patients too, if given the right direction, can minimize intervention and find long-term ways of coping with the problem. This applies even to chronic issues like diabetics and infertility - if one knows the way to root health with Oneness as the fundamental principle, then there is a differentiation of that which leads towards health and that which leads away from it. The issue for medicine is about making this a clear expression to patients, so they can see which way their instinct takes them. This is possible, if there is a sense of medical Oneness.

One of the worst problems with modern medicine is prognostics. The prognostic process is utterly brutal and narrow-minded. If a prognostic session was energetically understood, it would be banned by the World Health Organization. The process of expressing to a patient his/her life expectancy and whether something is curable or incurable is totally tied up with the way these doctors think about medicine. As a result, the options they have are slim and the consequences are passed on to the patient. The psychological binding of this process has such severe implications, such as panic and distress, that they are the last thing you would want for a person who is very sick. This inevitably creates a domino-effect of anxiety and depression, which leads to further pathological implications, as the body is totally unified. It is utterly insensitive and totally unresponsive of practitioners to lack the understanding that everything they express and all they do with a patient has an effect. This is the mechanism of "belief" within medicine which can be used to entice a healing or, in "black magic" which is what a "bad prognosis" is really, induces a further aggression of symptoms based on the belief and fear of the doctor being passed on. Primal medicine is beyond belief, it is beyond placebo and does not have the hierarchical ideology that one could be fooled either way by a practitioner, but rather is about intrinsic sense of innate health and a return to this within. New emerging quantum physics would agree with the damage of prognostics as would the newly-emerging areas of psycho-neuro-immunology and the mind-body doctors who are beginning to grasp some of the ancient principles within the Newtonian ideology, but medicine is still in a non-observational capacity, still seeing patients as items on a factory floor, to be shelved and categorized.

All this does is keep us in "factory" mode. Prognostics is the first and most obvious aspect of medicine where it is best to say "I don't know" rather than "I know, and this is what will happen." Inevitably, this sends patients who are easily influenced, rather than sense-based, more rapidly towards a grave already marked out for them. The doctor's mind and ideas are so limited, as to often be considered irrelevant, except in the most severe and most obvious of situations, and even then they have sometimes been proved wrong. If one wants a broad view of something, it is best not to go towards people who use microscopes to look at the world. Unfortunately, this is the present case, with a great number of doctors and those in the bio-medical field, as it is in the "leaves-view" of medicine where things are separate, cut and dried. The Oneness at the background is missed, due to focusing so heavily on the symptoms rather than on the life-force that is propelling them.

It is important to note that I am focusing on the medical model rather than specific practitioners, who may well go beyond the paradigms of their methodology in order to cure, rather than to be purely and coldly clinical, as is the nature of this form of medicine. When a patient is truly dying, this becomes clear through the course of treatment and acceptance can naturally follow, if the basis for the approach is engendering awareness. In all the cases I have seen where a patient was told about the fact they were dying, in appropriate circumstances, it was absolutely obvious to the patient what was going on and already a process of acceptance was occurring - it was not imposed. Doctors should be clear as to when to explain the situation, and only do so when they know the life-force of the patient is at an end. The whole idea of life-force is not understood or acknowledged in this situation, it becomes the spread of a pathological idea of being separate. In Ancient medicine, it is only when life-force is broken or there is no root energy in the body that the patient will die, and even at this time one needs to appropriately consider the situation - and what causes great distress is the least useful, most unnatural thing to do at this time.

The leaves of the medical tree are seasonal. They are dependent on the nutrients reaching the very top, but if they pull too strongly on their resources then the whole tree will die, in just one season. This is expressed in the oil crisis which is now upon us, which indicates simply that we must move towards sustainability and unity.

Richard Dawkins and modern conservatism in the context of the pure- science of ancient energetics

Richard Dawkins is one of the world's most famous spokespersons for the "public face of science" and so the following addresses the views of all who share his way of thinking. I have researched his theory and ideology, which, like that of numerous other people who are arguing about energetic medicines, comes from a huge lack of personal experience and a huge requirement for their idea of "science" to be right and overcome all, much like a highly dogmatic religion. I have focused on the following argument, for clarity of content, and specifically on Dawkins' assertions made in his Channel 4 film in 2007: "Enemies of Reason", in Part 1: "Slaves to Superstition", in which Dawkins looks at the whole New Age movement and in Part 2: "The Irrational Health Service", in which Dawkins gives his opinion about the various forms of natural therapy. Dawkins' main assertion is that he is a scientist, first and foremost, and so it is here, with his initial background premise, that I hold serious contention with him. Science, in its truest terms, is about the attempt to go beyond the subjective view and into the objective, and it is here that Dawkins fails, from the beginning. As with most people who hold very strong views, Dawkins sees what he wants to see regarding what science is, and as a result produces a completely skewed view for others to grapple with. Dawkins' viewpoint is deeply aligned with Newtonian physics at its basis. The principles of Newtonian physics revolve greatly around the physical form. Although it was not Newton who focused the mind towards physical structures being absolute phenomena (interestingly he is likely to have been also interested in esoteric alchemy!), he certainly formed theories which were about the measurability of energy based in physical or some-thing, rather than no-thing, or the field which lies between the parts or between the energetic bodies. This drove science - and so biology, and inevitably medicine - to a physical-only policy, which is still prevalent today.

In the ancient and particularly Eastern context, there is total unity between the physical and the energetic, between the energy of something and its transformation into energy and back into matter, and also the background no-thing that is the canvas on which it is all happening. In general, one could say that Newtonian mechanics is "useful" only in a world of humans that accept its viewpoint. It created the Industrial Revolution and the whole basis of the world of mechanisation which we have today; we have seen and are living within the age old world view of dualism but from the Newtonian perspective.

Quantum theory and its movement towards a yet-illusive "Unified theory of everything", as its name suggests is aimed much more at the all-inclusiveness of all phenomena. It attempts to unify all phenomena, and as such, it moves closer towards the ancient understanding. We have not yet seen a world developed out of a quantum world view - a world based in unified connection rather than separation - which would inevitably draw us to far more natural ways of being. The point is that while energetic medicine sees non-duality, modern medicine sees duality, and since dualism is either something or something else, it is always "some-thing" that is focused on. This tends to always be a physical substrate of some kind, and so modern medicine is bound and confined to the physical; ancient medicine, on the other hand, sees the whole as an accumulation and expansion of energy on a boundless background.

Although Dawkins accepts that to know and understand quantum physics is something that is beyond him, he continues to peddle Newtonian ideology, which he knows is out of date.

Although one could argue that because quantum physics hasn't yet found the absolute universal theory they are after, it is impossible for biologists or chemists or those at the upper levels of the science model to use the new theory. However, I feel that if it is known in the mind of the physicist, who is really the captain of the scientific ship, that the foundation principle is not absolute, this to some level needs to feed doubt into the minds of the chemists and biologists that indeed they are not seeing the whole picture and that at any moment the whole universe could change. The issue we can see with conservatism is that there is rigidity, so until there is theoretical proof within Newtonian dynamics, an argument will not be accepted. Interestingly, this means that, like Wittgenstein's "a fly in a bottle", the Newtonian can't actually find his way out of his own parameters, he can't see the broader viewpoint. Therefore he is unlikely to accept a whole new science where the mechanistic methods of the past are seen as fragments of a much larger understanding, which is what quantum mechanics is attempting to see. This should, at the very least, make science less sure of itself, but it does not.

The current difficulty is that the model one is working with cannot be seen from any angle other than the one it was based on. The base ideologies of physics have affected everything, all the way up the chain to biology, from the quark and lepton of the inner atom. Dawkins' assertion, therefore, based where it is, is not only overtly coarse and simplistic, but what he suggests is like considering how to paint your ceiling while the builders are removing the carpet from under you! This being the case, Dawkins' assertions, arguments and experimentation based on the so-called accuracy of "double blind" trials and so on, are blind to their own foundational ideology, their very premises have not been considered. Dawkins is then left speaking through limitations, while also knowing that the quantum physicist

146

potentially knows something that can overturn his entire world view - but he can't understand that person, as they talk in code. Interestingly, energetic medicine is a similar code and it is also why quantum physicists often lean towards ideas and concepts associated with the very ancient ideas in healing. People like Deepak Chopra, Fritjof Capra and Gary Zukav often talk about the crossovers. However, I agree with Dawkins that emphasizing the similarity of these two regions is useless and actually creates deep confusion. Far from being like modern physics, ancient energetic understanding is far beyond modern physics. The so-called understanding of modern physics is like an adult-child playing with a toy and not quite understanding the "toy" is their own hand, relative to the all-inclusiveness of the expression of Universal Oneness and energetic flux known through the sensitivity of our experience and expressed in ancient energetic medicine.

Dawkins is right when he says we can't use the language of energetics and modern science together, they do need to be clearly viewed in order to be presented as background and foreground respectively. However, he fails to understand his own limitation, stuck in mechanistic paradigms that block his view of a broader understanding. When this eventually does break through in physics, this will undermine his underlying premises and so his statements will fall like a house of cards. It is really interesting when biology and quantum mechanics start to blend and biologists accept different ideas about what they are seeing. An example of this is Dr. Rupert Sheldrake and his understanding of what he called the "morphogenic field" associated with biological life. Also, the work of Bruce Lipton completely alters our understanding of biology and starts to allow us another view into quantum-biology, which essentially isn't biology any more, as quantum physics has the potential to obliterate divisions between fields of science and art for that matter. "Fields of science" again is a fragmented Newtonian model. Dawkins expresses that we are living in a world where we ought to be in awe of pharmaceutical drugs and the industry that formulates them, as we have become complacent about the fact that externally- contracted diseases, like small pox, mumps and measles hardly exist at all now, due to the "power" of Western medical treatment. He also expresses that the quality of life has gone up and people are living longer. Here, quantity is the key ideal and quality is not understood. Like an economic model of Spencer, Dawkins' version of science is something that is a "fixer", a simple DIY issue, which has been getting more and more efficient.

However, the modern approach focuses on the symptoms of disease, not the cause of dis-ease, which Deepak Chopra brilliantly suggests has much more to do with the "fear of death" than anything else. All that has happened is that now people are suffering and dying of internally-sourced diseases, rather than externally-influenced disease. Internal diseases like cancer, heart disease, depression, and auto-immune disease have become prolific, while mumps and measles have taken a dive as a result of immunisation. Interestingly, something that is not mentioned is that all of these diseases which required intervention of modern methods were associated with livestock breeding and mono-culture which was based in agriculture, leading to the industrial revolution. It is the fact that most epidemics associated with humans have been because nature has been looked away from and humans have forcibly taken a hand in "taking control" of nature or sanitizing it, thereby witnessing an energetic balancing effect in massive widespread disease. Even without seeing this, the issues are the same; still, the energy of dis-ease has been transferred from exterior to interior-generated focus. Dawkins will probably retort, of course, that science hasn't got there yet, but just like a rainbow which his science can never reach, it is always about symptom-seeking and attempting to find the "solution", rather than seeing what is provided within nature, unabated by human mind-identification.

To take the intention out of modern ways of science is to clearly move back to a pure-science, a science of pure rationality, in fact. When the observer is no longer involved in the experiment, he becomes a naturalist, in a similar way that Darwin "discovered" and others "discovered." Discovery is honest, it means it was there beforehand, not pre-intended or from a sought-out direction, but instead something became clear as a result. In fact when people deeply let go they "discover" the "I" or lack of it! People discovering aspects of the world around them - this is the way of pure-science - it has no intended direction and simply sees what is. If, however, science is taken over by intention, one must find the root of this intention to find the bias. For example, geneticists attempting to find the cure for cancer first need to ask, "Why am I doing this?" If the answer is "to save people" or "to stop people dying of this dreadful disease" then we must ask, "Why is it dreadful?" The answer is usually "because people die of it." Then the retort is, "What's wrong with death?" And in the end, we find that the basis of this "science" is a moralistic or ethical view about death, based on personal fear. This is actually the same way that Spencer, and social commentators/writers like Thomas Hobbs before him, moulded biology and how Dawkins affects science; all are based on these personal assertions. If you want pure objectivity, you need to be open to the result. Therefore, pure-science in the modern age is very rare and perhaps only confined to those "naturalists" still left, who are truly rational in their way of seeing natural phenomena.

It must be made clear what a scientist is, in relation to a user of scientific knowledge. A pure-scientist is a naturalist, looking at what is and making notes on it. This is all about scientific discovery. Those who use science, however, are the engineers - most of modern medicine comes under this category. Those who create technologies and industries, including the pharmaceutical industry, are not scientists in pure-rational terms, they are engineers. Even in the formulation of an experiment to find out "X" or "Y" specifically, there is intervention and it therefore has the basis of engineering, not of science. Even at the genetic level we know these people for what they are: "genetic engineers." We must be careful to see the pure science and the true scientist quite separately from the rest of the rat-race of industry and its "intention" which is all about other "intentions" and hypotheses built on still further "intentions", not about observing things as they are, like Darwin did. There are those scientists who intuitively know something and write it down, only to later discover that they were right. These people, for example Albert Einstein, prove undeniably that they are connecting to something larger than themselves when inspired to create. That unknowable sense is intuition. So it seems that the scientist can observe, when being him/herself, and find the whole universe - or observe the outside and know the whole of him/herself.

Here is the paradox of pure-science. "Proof" is a way of looking at something specific, rather than an absolute totality; science needs to be humble in relation to a greater, broader viewpoint. This should soon be coming within quantum theory. If the aim of science is to see objectively, to reveal the "mind of God" so to speak, then two issues must be taken seriously by all who proclaim to be scientists. If one is rational, it is important not to do science with an intended effect. To attempt to do anything, in fact, will cause an effect in the experiment, as modern physics has demonstrated time and again. So if one can't help but involve oneself in the experiment, what can be done in order to attain data and to understand? The closest we can get is pure and unadulterated observation. This is what Darwin attempted in his life with some success. However, this concept seems to have eluded Dawkins. The observation of nature is all we can "do" without influencing or agitating the issue and turning science into Dawkins-science, or David-science for that matter; the subjective needs to be avoided. All the ancient understanding actually comes from this pure-science, the science of observation and sensing. Some would call this a "radical" empiricism. To see things as they are is what science was originally about. At the time, it was not called science, but philosophy, "the love of wisdom." Here, science and art and life were all one, there was no separation.

For many years now, science has been carried by industry, by politics, and by the subjectivity of Dawkins and others. This delivers an argument much more based on personal ideals and life history, rather than observational rationalism. The second premise of pure-science is really to complete itself, and this is clearly and brilliantly explained in the work of Douglas Harding. Harding explains that science cannot be complete if it just looks outwards without acknowledging the one who is looking. The observer is the fundamental basis upon which the observation is made. As Harding explains, to literally look back towards the observer is the only way of being sure of total objectivity. This requires the openness of the observer, an openness to what they will find, without a pre-determined idea. If science even partially followed the two premises above, it would be a thousand times more than what we see today, which is a huge group of people with ideas they have been taught about "how things are," basing more ideas on top of these and then suggesting that this is the only true way. In fact, they have created the very thing that they wish to avoid - bigotry and religious dogma, as Dawkins exemplifies. It is especially amusing that the very premises on which they build their ideas can, with a moment's notice, be totally contextualized by the ever-broadening effect of the ideas of modern physics, which are making it very unstable to be a Newtonian any longer. "*The Field*" by Lynne McTaggart is a book which goes into this kind of ideology, but still this has stayed with the ancient understanding, due to its belief that what is being discovered is something new. It is only something new to the few looking at it today, but to those who study the ancient material this way has been trodden for thousands of years.

Dawkins proclaims that there was no golden age of wisdom, and I agree - just a context which we have forgotten and given up for the details. Dawkins believes we have progressed, but the key point is that there has been no progression, no formulation of anything different at the base of things. Only the surface has changed - the symptoms have changed place. Now they are inside more than outside. Still, the driving force of the human being is to live anxiously and in fear; these things have not changed and are the key root of the dis-ease process. It may be that science is looking for an "answer," but my feeling is that it is actually chasing its own tail. The very thing driving the scientific search outwards in observation is due to a belief in what's "out there" as being the truth, rather than what they have lost, that which makes the ancient way a complete and pure-science, namely that the observer is the key part of the puzzle. After this is found, science as we understand it today completely loses its meaning, because it is fundamentally based on separation and dualism. The interesting thing is that when science actually finds what it is looking for, in a deep sense, it will actually end itself, in much the same way as Wittgenstein ends philosophy by looking at the root of words being used. In the end, peace and Oneness will always prevail, no matter how hard the scientist looks outwards. Just as in Stanley Kubrick's masterpiece, 2001: A Space Odyssey, if the scientist looks outwards to the edges of what is known, he simply finds Him/Her-Self.

Dawkins' attempts to move into other areas like religion, morality, ethics and so on are all a part of his quest for "rationality," which is his own brand of materialistic religion. Again the argument is the same, which is that if the initial premise of an argument is unfounded then there is no argument, and this is where we started with Dawkins and others of his disposition. His eccentricity skews his view, and he will be lost in a spiral of continual "war," which is exactly what Western medicine and science has been drawn into - a war with everything, including itself. This war is the dis-ease itself, it is the conflict and the problem. But when you are in the wood, you can't see the trees. From the perspective of Oneness, Dawkins can be seen for exactly what he is, a part of Oneness, but a part that believes itself to be separate and at war. This provokes his animosity and his lack of acknowledgment of others who could provide him with a broader viewpoint, if he was able to consider it.

What Dawkins concedes to "the placebo effect" is something fudged, a fudge factor that keeps on lingering, which neither he nor other scientists can identify as a quantifiable or qualifiable issue. It is, in fact, an energetic issue and the same issue that is irritating the quantum physicist and everyone else. Dawkins focuses on the theoretical, not the healing process, the idea rather than the sensitivity to what is, the mind as opposed to the senses. If the human can cut himself off from everyone, as Dawkins expresses in his "selfish gene" ideology, war and violence and further processes demonstrating the lack of unity are bound to follow. In his argument, however, he expresses that a lot of the people involved in natural therapies are plagiarizing or are charlatans and are involved in belief systems, not medicine. Actually, this is true. A huge number of the people trained in natural therapies who invent, practise, and express images and ideas about healing, are just "doing a job" in a conventional way, as is true of any industry, or they are there for the hierarchical power and/or financial reward. The ideas have no feeling, no particular interest or connection to them. These people should not be practising, it is simply not "themselves" to express such a thing. However, there are also those who sense and who feel, often in a totally unique way, and the explanation of what they are sensing is totally baffling, because it is offered in ideas and words. However, like ten descriptions of the taste of honey, there will be a quality that is universal, even if the explanations are totally different.

Medical Oneness is about finding this common language and understanding things "as they are." It is a foundation for the renewal of true, pure, radically empirical science, rather than irrational ideology such as Dawkins'. Much like the establishment he works for and upholds, and as in Orwell's classic "*Nineteen Eighty-Four*", the Ministry of Peace is actually the Ministry of War, and the Ministry of Provision is the ministry of Taxation. In the world of Dawkins, the Ministry of Rationality hides the Ministry of Irrationality, the Ministry of Objectivity is the Ministry of Subjectivity, and the Ministry of "Cure the Cause" is the Ministry of "Affecting the symptoms." If we see biomedicine in context, we find its use and its benefits rather than its all-encompassing control. Immunization and antibiotics and other very effective ideas are useful and effect change in the short term, in the acute. Yes, even immunization we could call a short-term medical ideology, the effect of adding an irritant to the body, which the body's immune system responds to and cathartically discharges seems brilliant. Humans survive longer, and more humans live. This seems good, and this seems the ideological basis, but of course all that it changes is a population size which increases and increases. Also, this is inaccurate, pre-historic humans used to live to the same kinds of ages we are living today, however infant mortality rate was higher (although there were many more births per mother) so when averaging statistics has for many years been considered that pre-historic life was very short, this is not the case (Ryan C., Jethá C.(2010), p.200).

The process of forcefully preventing an illness or death creates a longer-term effect of doing further damage to one another and the planet's resources. If we look and see what actually is, if we work with what there is rather than trying to manipulate, if we treat the dis-ease as it comes and work alongside natural selection and respect it, if we respect death instead of fearing it, then we are truly living in a natural way. Medicine, which interferes in natural processes, is bound to find itself tangled in a much larger issue at the end. Long-term effects of any changes we are making will be written indelibly in our gene pool. We may, in the long term, see immunization, for example, become the very death warrant for a huge percentage of the world's population. We have no way of finding this out now, but intervention never comes without re-balancing, yin and yang always find balance. Darwin's brilliance, in contrast, is that he never intervened, he just observed and noted. When something is so effective that it kills all bacteria, you know there will be a repercussion somewhere down the line, in that the bacteria are part of us, and we are part of them. Natural medicine goes with the way nature is going, it doesn't force or pre-empt, but considers what is and predicts from here. Blanket treatments and universally using single medicines for whole populations is as barbaric as giving everyone the same close shave, even if their jaw and neck are a different shape!

The difficulty is in understanding what it is that medicine can do, what sustainability and medicine have in common. It is also difficult to see what all this has to do with the true reasons for us getting this far down the track of mis-aligning our fears with scientific study - the two are totally different. The fear that drives the whole industry of medicine and the fear that creates medicines like immunization, antibiotics, and other fragmentary drugs, propels the ideas with it. The drugs are imbued with this quality of energy and as such are not relevant in naturalism, natural selection, or sensitivity. The bitter pill that Dawkins will eventually need to swallow is that while human beings believe they are adapting very well to their environment, they are not doing so at all; they are using the dis-ease pattern of mind-identification itself to attempt to alleviate the suffering. Einstein's point rings true again and again: the problem is not being looked at other than from the ideology that created it. This is a key, the context and broader view of the implications of the so-called "magic" bio-medicines need to be understood deeply before they are considered as perfect, ideal and balanced products. In fact, once again we find the opposite being true, but the truth is hard to take if you really want to get down to the base-line of what is going on.

This means that all is acceptable as a form of medicine, not just the physical tools, like surgery, but also the healer's touch, or even healing without touch, and the subtleties which physicality is too dense to be useful for. The interaction of the accumulated and dense and the subtle, expansive and energetic is the realm of the healer, who is between and involved in both. Medical Oneness can only be seen from Oneness, non-dualism. If we are stuck in the Newtonian physicality, we will only be able to diagnose and see in these terms, which results in modern culture and all those who have association with it literally and metaphorically buying into either its dualism or its individualism, both of which are one expression. We are increasingly blind to our senses, with machines often exacerbating this. We see everything with a border and boundary, not the true perspective of a blurring of boundary (for none in reality exist), and unity with all of life, innate in the view of the infant. These ideologies are gradually being overthrown by the scientific community as being too simplistic and mechanistic. Newer models have arisen, which attempt to find universal principles of the universe, which is now the realm of quantum physics.

Until the ancient ideals and modern physics find their unity, it will be very difficult for doctors to accept the explanation in this book as a foundation for investigation in medicine. Sensory or radical-empiricism, as a foundation for medicine, has not been the majority idea since the Taoists of China and the Greeks and the Indian doctors of Ayurvedic medicine or the indigenous medicine of the many nations of the world. Today there are still traces of this background in the midst of our foreground focusing, but it is very hard to come by unless one knows where to look. Pure observation is a lost sense and this is what is deeply lacking in us and our lives. The mind cannot be calmed and inevitably we lose relaxed-concentration to sense. However, the ancient threads to this are around us, in the newly-named ideas and fragmented ideologies of the "New Age" medicine, even right up to the modern medicines at the "top of the tree." The need to return Home or to a place outside of dis-ease is fundamental, whatever the culture or creed, there is total Oneness in this evaluation.

The question really is: do humans, at this point in history, want to look at themselves and pure-science directly, or do they prefer to be blinkered in such a way as to be afraid of death? The latter preference leads to the process of living becoming about avoidance. Fear of death is not instinctual, as could be concluded by people who truly observe nature. No animal is afraid of an idea, for there is no idea of death. Only humans hold onto this notion and so live in this delusion. This is hard reality, pure reason, rationality. This is the truth of it, but Dawkins actually looks the other way and hides behind fear of loss, as to some degree is the general human condition.

The GP enigma

If only it were the case that the general practitioner was "general". The bulk of what I have been expressing about the "upper leaf-branch-focused" medicine is not that there is anything wrong with being a specialist or "leaf"-interested, but that in being this one also loses the connection with the general or background-root perspective. One loses why one is focusing so intently and specifically, thereby losing the reason for treatment. One gets absorbed by the microscopic and forgets the patient as a whole. One loses the reason for medicine in a mad panic to "save lives" at all costs. If practitioners who specialise keep the true general energetic principles intact at the root, they will know when the symptom they are so interested in is acute and needs to be dealt with immediately or is chronic and therefore needs to be treated by a practitioner who deals with the general patterns, not the symptoms. This is a good specialist. A general practitioner, therefore, is really a practitioner who treats the root of disease and does not touch the symptoms. This practitioner is based on the sage-like ideology of Christ or Buddha, truly reaching the heart of the problem. This, however, is a far cry from what a general practitioner is today. The GP focuses on symptoms and then refers the patient to someone else, who focuses more intently on a specific symptom. No one in modern medicine looks at the root of the issue, and this is why it is a medicine forgetting its roots. It desperately needs to be re-rooted, as do the natural therapies in the "New Age" section because as we have seen the movement has a tendency to go upwards and inwards rather than downwards and outwards. The part of the tree of medicine which is in touch with the root and has its branches flourishing is root-based medicines. Individuals have no place in the general principles of medicine, individual expression naturally occurs and this is just the way it is, but this is not the foundations of medicine. Focus needs to be on that which is universally true. If what is universally true can be agreed upon, then it is possible that individuality can be contextualized and a different future developed. In order to move towards a future of sustainability and "paradise," we need to truly allow nature to lead, with the inner sense in primal medicine and the outer sense in an awareness like Feng Shui /permaculture and expressions of this nature. It is key to base one's expression on the overall whole. It is not about different viewpoints, it is about finding the origin or centre of that viewpoint, looking to the essence of the viewer him/herself and questioning what is back at the centre.

The outer world is formed by the connection we have to the inner world. If the connection to the inner is lost, we are lost in the foreground of life, battered by the tide. But at the root, if there is reliance on senses, then there is a true connection, a realization of origin. This may be philosophical, but it is simply an expression of what is. In medicine, if this becomes more noticed, what follows is the realization of the root and unity of the medical tree, rather than a top-heavy expression. Understanding and acknowledging one's senses in diagnosis and treatment, and feeling, rather than thinking, about the patient's situation, seeing connection rather than dissonance, this is the beginning of the end of the rootless tree. For each time we do this, we breathe life into ourselves as a Oneness of expression and existence and rooted energy in the essence of life. Hence, the background of life is Oneness, and the foreground is the body or form, which from the perspective of separation seems like an individual. Oneness is simply One with All. From this perspective, life has endless possibility.

chapter 7

Transition Medicine:
the realization - seeing past
separation to Oneness

The change that is gradually occurring naturally over time is quite an obvious one, it is the movement back towards nature. For some, this will be a heart-wrenching experience of being faced with dead-ends in every direction, such as the fuel crisis looming. For others, it will be a process of realizing one cannot use force and that eventually nature is the underpinning unity. Individualism is dying, even if right now it looks as if it is stronger than ever; in fact, this strength is based on increasingly shaky foundations. Peak oil and the financial and industrial collapse of capitalistic ideology is inevitable and has been predicted for years; whether peak oil is five years or a hundred years off, it makes no difference. The point is, whether we like it or not, things are changing. Individualism - the ideology of the separate self - has to come to an end. Therefore, this moment in our understanding is a time of transition. There is a process by which we are leaving the towns and moving back to nature, leaving the factories and moving towards hand-made, simpler ways of being. This is very gradual, almost imperceptible, but soon it will be clear that it is inevitable. Medicine will be part of that change, and so medicine will need to be sustainable. It will need to see life and death as a continuum, with the fear and the taboos taken out of the process of dying. Gradually, as the human once again becomes a part of nature, we will find ourselves back in the place we once called home - Eden - finding that we never left but only thought we did.

At this moment, however, there is a huge dilemma: the older generations are often stuck in an uncompromising, individualist ideal and the younger generations have no root yet and seem to have no future. There is a big question mark in the air. Here is where transition begins. Transition is the movement from a place of assurance in that what one is doing is "right" or "just" or "positive" or "my personal expression" to a realization of a larger plane of existence. This stage in between is quite disconcerting as one realizes, often with dismay, but sometimes with great relief, that what one thought all along to be true and that which one's whole life was "based" on, has falseness to it, or is a mask to something behind. This is not to say that the mask doesn't exist, but rather that the mask is not the inner and deep expression. It is a superficial expression and as such is secondary to the root, it is a branch of that which came before. Once the root is acknowledged in whatever way, the root of Oneness, then things change on the surface, and the mask is often renounced. Or instead, it becomes the true face of humanity, undistorted by belief or by dualistic tendency. The transition is often painful, almost a re-birthing of sorts. For the medical profession, this is just beginning. It is the difficulty of realizing that the ancients did have something that is now lost and that this missing background quality is deeply needed, in order to allow medicine to be sustainable in the future. For the "New Age" medicines, it is the realization that styles have no real importance and occur without effort, if one is rooted in the principle of Oneness. Since this must occur, they will eventually be in communication and community with one another. The transition is from being an individual to becoming part of the Oneness, from separating towards joining. This is done from within, rather than from without, although often the first brings about the second. Each person individually needs to sense for themselves whether they wish to live from the source of the expression living through them or from an ec-centric, off-centre perspective, where they are drawn into illusions of charity, or support intertwined with capitalistic individualism and so on. All are the same quest, in fact, which is believing and living in the exterior world, unrooted, and so bound to its "prosperity," which is actually great poverty in disguise. One still has not accepted the here and now moment, where there is nothing that gets better than this moment.

The move to what I have called "transition medicine" is, to start with, a move towards chaos, a point where one doesn't know what works anymore. One can begin to see this in modern medical practices, often in the more expensive parts of cities where "integrative medicine" is starting up. These are clinics involving modern Western medicine and including all sorts of other practitioners as well, all in the same space. This is supposed to provide a complete picture of healing resources, but is far from doing that. "Integrative" here is just an umbrella idea which holds a lot of parts under one name. They are still separate parts. Referral is hardly understood because each person in the clinical setting is seen to be separate, diagnosing and talking in separate, root-less languages about the patients. This is not integrating anything, in fact, it is more and more confusing to the patient,

163

who has no idea where to turn. Everyone's business card tells you that the treatment is holistic, yet unity of understanding does not exist. Rather, it becomes a situation of "my holism is better than your holism" which is, of course, totally individualistic. The process should always be about seeing the background and not getting lost in the foreground. This is what is missing in all areas of medicine, from the most clearly individualistic to the most seemingly energetic. However, "integrative medicine" is the transition point, and although some of us have our eyes on a unified understanding and a connection back to nature, this will be a journey that not everyone comes to see so quickly. One has to descend into the chaotic, from "I know" to "I thought I knew, but now I'm not sure" to: "I don't know, but I trust" to "I am, that I am." These four stages of expression are what transition medicine is all about.

Ancient diagnostics and the idea of using this as a fundamental language in healing, in order to identify and speak to one another, will draw us constantly deeper and deeper into this cohesive unity of sustainable medicine. As humans become closer to nature and move away from industry, this unity of sustainable medicine will naturally cohere with a lifestyle and way of existing that is at peace, rather than at war. This changes the nature of the very disease itself. Transition medicine, as a movement, acts like a long-required catharsis for modern medicine. The structures that once held it up start to break down and the industry and economy that power it end up falling with it. The doctor-on-high, who sees people into the world and out of the world, is no longer seen as the master of life and death, but simply like all the rest of the people, as an expression of healing, of which birth and death are just aspects. In fact, birth and death, which are seen as events which should take place in hospitals, are not diseases, but natural happenings. There is no master, nature is that which is followed, going with its flow. The youth and the aged are seen as a whole, old age once again becomes about acceptance and wisdom in the ways of natural expression of being, rather than a situation where the old are discarded and useless; the only reason for this is that the old have ceased to be wise, in general, or their wisdom is missed and not considered.

Looked at from a broader picture, we can see that the process of understanding medical Oneness is not a problem of East versus West, or Modern versus Ancient. In fact, everyone has always sensed the root movement towards healing. What we are acknowledging is not that one aspect is "useless" and another is "better" but that the ancient perspective sheds light on our current situation. It allows us to remember our original questions, or our original sense of what medicine is all about and why we are practising it, rather than following tangents of thought that lead us further and further away from wholeness. Wholeness is, in fact, all of our "goals".

The benefits and the mis-fits of transition medicine

The initial transition is into chaos, and then out of chaos into clarity. Through this process, medicine transforms. Transformation is not just incremental change, it is a total transformative process. The process for this change to take place is downwards and outward rather than upwards and inwards this can be explained as follows:-

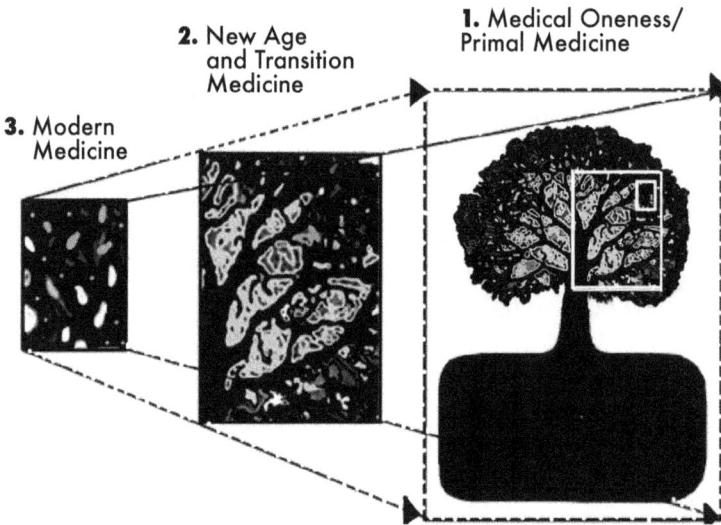

What this would actually do to modern medicine is quite considerable. The process of being able to see the whole medical tree allows things to be placed into context deeply. As you can see the process is a reversal of this book. To begin we started with ancient medicine but this is our end point here. Transition medicine is really in the place of the "New-Age", in a way the chaos of individualistic perspectives on a movement towards wholeness. The process we see from 3 to 1 is a change in the suppleness of the mind. It is about letting go and relaxing, it is in fact the process of healing, a transition from the contracted and dis-ease state of specialization and focusing to the expanded platform of medicine as a whole, intensely focusing in to the top of the tree causing a top-heavy attitude and an ego-centric outlook - as we expand out things fall naturally into place and there is less and less fear.

From this simple diagram above we can at last let go of the idea that we need to get a "modern perspective" on things. So many of the stylistic models we have looked at are formulated by modern day practitioners and are theories which see a practical view based in the individual's limitation, instead of looking to the background view of the primal and also ancient basis of medicines. This ends the idea that somehow we need to improve on what went before or even put it into "up-to-date" terms for the modern era, or make it more "practical", "pragmatic" or alter it in any way at all. The Primal principles have always been there in the present movement, within the practitioner's innate knowing of how to heal without being taught a thing - simply instinctual sense. The modern view as expressed above is a partial view and as such is a contraction that needs to be let go of for there to be a Oneness in medicine or in anything at all. Modern ideas are not a "waste of time" but they are partial, not "bad" or "good" but they <u>are</u> partial and however one looks at it this means that the background Oneness is hard to see from this limitation. It is of course always present but just hard to see. Letting go of modern idealism leads to a sensory understanding of the primal nature of being, this is as in-the-moment as it is ancient; in fact, just as in so many of the writings from the ancient times, there truth speaks as loud today as it did in antiquity, and the indigenous peoples that still connect to this simplicity are too a living representation of primal institute medicine in today's world. It is like a layer of freshly cut grass on a field and the stalks that remain connected to the earth that have not been severed , these are the indigenous peoples and the grasses of ancient wisdom still alive in the midst of our feeling of disconnection.

Practically what this will do is peoples whose notions and ideologies will change. As an expanded view comes into play it pulls away the very foundations of the social norms we see around us. When this occurs the requirement for medicine of a specific kind starts to evaporate because the notion of medicine has changed at its root with the practitioners. When it changes here this message is passed on and gradually everyone gets a sense of inner rather than "sought-after" health. There is a total change, a collapse of society as we know it, but towards a peaceful and sustainable living. As explained before we are not really looking at the tools of medicine - whether it is a scalpel, infra-red lamp, moxibustion, a needle, oils or the hands and body energy that is being used, this is inconsequential - what is really important is the theoretical paradigm that focuses and detects the use of these things. When this changes, immediately the amount of prescribed medication for chronic patients would immediately reduce and the "alternative therapies would be seen to be able to deal with this much better. The medical systems we know as being modern medicine would become acute-physical medicine used in serious accident and injury as a primary basis. Most chronic dis-ease would be looked at in the form of suffering and the reduction of this as key to health. This would be a flip-turn in social workings. As a result the balance would shift from mind and contraction and inward dis-ease, to expansion and non-separateness, an opening outwards and downwards toward the body and feet as opposite to the head.

So the people who will really lose their jobs are those in the drug companies, as that market will crash. There is nothing that can be done to "save" this situation. They must use their resources in other ways, drawing towards ideologies of sustainability, so economies-of-scale do not transgress into the refuge of natural healing. This is vitally important. Healing is not about man-made ideologies of "survival" and is rooted in the objectivity of science - this science is one that is not led by human mind-identification, but by nature. It looks back at its origin and is not out to find the fragment, it is ancient-science that is one with nature. Patients want doctors back, they do not want the machines. People connect to people, if we put something in the way we will always cause separation and isolation, and in the end this is dis-ease. Another way to consider this is moving into the context and background, which is especially moving towards the earth and the ground again, rather than towards the head and the clouds. We humans have our heads in the clouds and as a result we lose our connection with the Mother Earth that is our foundation and root. This is a reality in every sense of what we find around us. If this is recognized, then transformational change can occur. To heal healing we must speak a unified diagnostic language of energetics.

The natural entropy towards ancient medicine

*"The confusion and consternation sets in
when we fail to see that one facet of our
lives is nestled into another, and that into
the next, and so on, creating our whole
system of being, completely interactive and
inclusive."*

Shirley Ann Jones, from "Simply Living"

*"An era can be considered over
when its basic illusions have been
exhausted"*

Arthur Miller

When we move through transition and find ourselves in a totally
new situation, which is at the same time very ancient, we are able
to re-discover that natural biorhythms and the human organism
are perfectly okay, when left alone by the mind-identification
process and the "tinkering" of the ideas we have about medicine.
Ancient medicine is the roots and earth, the background that
has been present all along, constantly open in its offering to re-
acknowledge itself, causing the idea of individual will or power to
fade into oblivion. This path through transition takes us from the
quietness of the university cloisters or the medical school in the
heart of the city where everything is known and clear, out of the
gates into the madness of city traffic and the chaos of the "real"
world, all the way through to where we reach nature at the outer
reaches of the town, and back home to the place where medicine
originated. This transition is the same for medicine itself. One
could call this a natural decay or entropy of the collapse of

society as it is now and our movement towards nature again - the dissolution of the "self." As we spend more time in the primal and the ancient ways their value becomes apparent, because they are unforced and less focused on alleviating pain; they are more about acknowledging the root and the dis-ease of the patient, helping them to see this in themselves and be independent of the doctor, in-fact for nature to be the doctor through them.

As we go on, the use for specialization reduces more and more. The machines become used less often, people return to sensing their bodies for themselves, and the doctor becomes less and less important, redundant and at peace. He/she eventually becomes a relic of a time when he/she was necessary, before the "enlightenment" of acknowledgment of dis-ease came about and people returned to nature. The doctor is now the emblem of the return to nature, the shaman with one foot firmly planted in the ground and the smallest of toes touching the city or town. The way home, the direction to centre, is what he/she can offer, but the path is not as one expects. It is about engaging with what is, not about forcing what is not. Natural entropy, if we follow the rhythms of the natural, will take us to natural medicine and to foundational context, for this is merely an explanation of the principles of instinct. The way medicine will transmute towards Oneness, once the ball starts to roll, will be through a process of decay of the old ways and transformation towards the new - which in fact is ancient. Medical Oneness therefore means the return to the energetic origin and the letting-go of the modern, for the primal understanding is eternal, while the modern is "fashion" and changes with the wind.

medical oneness

chapter 8

Medical Oneness:
the future possibility of medicine,
the sensitivity of the practitioner,
and the return *Home*

To be One, medicine has to come home to ourselves in this moment. There has to be an interest, or simply grace, to be at Centre, to sense our own senses and our own bodies. Shakespeare's "physician heal thyself" means to come back towards what one's senses are. To heal is to sense. Yinyang and the philosophy of Tao are about the true sense that we all share and know to be at a deep level. It is possible, even just for a moment, to see things in a different way. Look from where you are this moment, while reading these pages. What are you looking out of? What is it that you view the world from? Forget about what you look like in the mirror - look and see if there is anything there in your field of vision, not the pages and the room, but the other direction <u>towards</u> you. What's actually there? What is it that is the "you"? Interesting isn't it - that "you." It's a totally invisible no-thingness, a space. For all you know, you may not have a head. In fact, it would be correct to say that the true you, the essence of you, doesn't have a head. It doesn't have anything, but it is capacity for everything! So you are capacity for the whole world. Though this seems like a perspective shift, only a "little trick" of the senses, in fact this is reality, this is what we are missing.

When we touch another object or another person in healing, isn't it relevant that at a point where no force is applied, you can't tell where the object ends and where "you" begin? In listening, one can notice the silence behind the sound, a background which is there, no matter how loud the noise is. The background is that which the sound is formed from and goes back into when it dies down. That's the listener, listening. There is a taste that is a universal taste, which has no taste, behind the flavour of the foods you eat and smells you smell - it is odourlessness and tastelessness. It isn't bland or unpleasant, they are the background from which the tastes and odours appear within. This is the taster, tasting. All of our senses are doorways to Oneness, and all of these can be used in a healing context to sense and know what we're experiencing from a broader angle. Here, the whole pattern is known. To be a healer is to be sensitive, to be responsive and to be alive. It is not necessarily to "heal" in the sense of going through a process, but to heal the wounds of the ideas of obliviousness, of not being real, of being numb to instinct. It is about being and feeling with more tenderness and depth and sense than before - it's a desire for this, not a requirement. Those who want this become what they are, not what they are taught to be. A practitioner's radiance as someone who is in love with life and all of existence is the ideal in the ancient way. This radiance imbues patients with a sense that inspires movement towards the natural and away from the individual. It takes away from the personal and acknowledges the ever-present Oneness at the background of the world.

If we can see Oneness, then referral to other practitioners is obvious. The connection of patient to practitioner comes about and then, as a natural intuitive connection, we can sense when it is right that an individual needs to see a gentle female expression, a strong male expression, or a mix of male energy within female form or male within female form. Our energetic quality becomes key, over and above the skills we may possess and the tools we may use. Of course, restrictive theory will restrict what can be expressed, but in time these are displaced by life and the tools of practice are simply the instrument which best expresses the personality of the healer, in whatever form. When instrument and practitioner are clearly matched, it makes it clearer who they can help and why. Each expression is another aspect of ourSelf, or The Self. The clue is to come from Oneness. Then all the rest sorts itself out. Once the centre of the wheel is known, the wheel spins in its own way, one doesn't need to worry about the spokes. At long last, natural eco-systems of practice can develop. Instead of practitioners making referral to other practitioners, based on qualifications and guidelines, it will be more about a felt sense of what is right at any given time. A network for patient-centred, rather than practitioner-centred therapy can arrive only when the practitioners are interested in their own expression and "what they do best" in relation to the whole, i.e. colleagues practising differently. In the end, what we once saw as "limitation" of our practice can be seen as the point of referral, so we are actually sensing others around us as they truly are: fingers of the same hand, when it is the palm that is agreed and acknowledged. We need to understand that if, for example, we are overall yin in quality, then we will relate to and generally treat better, those patients of a similar nature to ourselves, and in the course of this, that allopathic treatment is the basis and homeopathic-cathartic is the branch practice. When our energetic base language is unified, health is truly "whole". Whichever way this is offered to the patient, the vessel that supplies the medicine needs to be acceptable to the patient's sensibilities. Opposite qualities of patient and practitioner will not resonate or understand one another.

This applies as well for living and working in the environment of therapists with totally opposite qualities. One needs to be clear about one's practice and one's expression and keep an environment that allows for this. Mixing opposites in any situation doesn't work in the long term. For acute situations, being around people who are very opposite to oneself can be very useful, but if the situation is chronic, then for example, in long-term treatment the best method is to find sameness. For patient to find practitioner or for referral networks to run well, the practitioner should know his/her expression intimately and understand it in relation to others. In this way small groups of practitioners can understand how they are similar and different from each other, where one can provide or where another would be more helpful. When everyone is speaking from the same music sheet then the music is unquestioned - the diagnostic language of primal medicine is the same, there is just a question of the right instrument for the right patient. This isn't about the arrogant attitude of "translating it" into terms he or she will understand better because they are an x, y, z practitioner, it is in fact a want to connect and realize that it is advantageous to speak the same language in treatment and to see beyond one's shell of ideologies and expand into a picture of Oneness that allows one to view the whole and one's part in it. It is both impersonal and intimate together. Far from the present commercial war, it is an eco-system of inter-relatedness and union, built on energetic understanding, not arbitrary pieces of paper. For sustainability this has to be our future, either through instinct now, or necessity later. Therefore, our sense energetically is not just towards and for the patient, but in every aspect of life, in sensing our role in the scheme of things, or how best we fit into a natural expression of the world at large. This process emanates from instinct and centre, nowhere else.

In concluding this book, I must point out again that it is not my individualistic vision that I am expressing. While it is easy to say that this work is a product of an idealist, full of his own personal desires for natural living, this would be to lose sight of the fundamental vision, which is not mine, but the vision of all of us who know there is the possibility of an openness leading back home to the true nature of Self. Oneness is the fundamental point at which we all stand, the singularity we are looking out from and the unconditional love that we are aware of in the background of the drama of existence. Lao Tzu, the Taoist sage, whose name means "old man," to conceal his identity so there was no deification and making the work unknown in origin, expresses this very vision in chapter 80 of his Tao Te Ching, "The Classic of the Way and Virtue":

> *Reduce the size of the population of the state.*
> *Though there are machines of war that are 10 or*
> *100 times greater than a single man, they are not*
> *needed. The people will be reluctant to travel long*
> *distances without reason for they know longevity.*
> *Even if they have ships and carts, they will have*
> *no use for them; weapons and amour have no*
> *occasion to be worn.*
> *Bring it about that people return to the use*
> *of knotting strings and using them, They will relish*
> *in their food, And in the beauty in their simple*
> *cloths, And will be content in their simple abode,*
> *And happy in the simplicity of natural existence.*

*Though neighboring states are within the sight
of one another, and the sound of dogs barking
and cocks crowing in one state can be heard
in another, yet the people of the one state will
grow old and die without having any dealings
withthose of another.*

(Modified from Lau D.C., 1964)

*"Human beings will be happier - not when they
cure cancer or get to Mars or eliminate racial
prejudice or flush Lake Erie, but when they find
ways to inhabit primitive communities again.
That's my utopia."*

Kurt Vonnegut, Jr.

An echo in recent times:-

*"The ability of Fourth world people to "keep
their feet on the ground" gives them knowledge
about the earth and her rhythms – information
required to remain human – that is only hinted
at in the city citizen's realm of knowledge"*

Dr. Rudolph Ryser

From more than 2,500 years ago, the same message has been
spoken. The message gets louder with every step we take away
from our centre and towards the horizon, and closer as we
acknowledge the very place we stand. The pushing forward, the
lack of contentment, the known angst of existence, and the dis-
ease that is its result, start to fade, and we are left free from the

possession that is mind-identity and individualism. A free man is an impossible notion, but freedom isn't. Individuals can't be free, for each finger of the hand cannot be separate from the others. As with all of humanity, there is a deep need to recognize its base for the very foundation of Itself and come home to the universal Oneness. Medical Oneness is an expression of this. It is still far from a problem-free ideology, but for those who would engage with the possibility of rooting themselves in yinyang or similar root principles there is no end to the possibilities of communication and the ability for which one can connect to others in this way.

Bill Mellison of the permaculture community says,

"The problems of the world are increasingly complex, the solutions, however, remain embarrassingly simple!"

And from the same community, Masanobu Fukuoka warns,

"If we throw Mother Nature out the window, she comes back in the door with a pitch-fork.".

"When one tugs at a single thing in nature, he finds it attached to the rest of the world." says John Muir, naturalist.

From Florence Nightingale:

"And as a wise man has said, no-one has ever done anything great or useful by listening to the voices from without." (Nightingale, 1859).

Fukushima Kodo, the acupuncturist, explains,

"Originally, medicine was a system of benevolent healing practices rooted in a tradition of neighbourly love."
(Fukushima, 1999).

I can think of no better way to re-connect to all of you than this expression, that of the words of one of the most famous healers of all time:

"Love thy neighbour as thyself." (Mark, 12:31)

Or perhaps, a better translation would be …

"Love; thy neighbour is thyself."

For more information please visit:

www.healthinstinct.org

medical oneness

Bibliography
Books, DVDs, Documentaries

- Alexander F.M. (1932), The Use of the Self, Orion Publishing

- Capra F., (1986), The Tao of Physics: An exploration of parallels between modern physics and Eastern mysticism, Flamingo- Collins Publishing Group, London.

- (DVD): Dawkins R., (2008) Rational Thought: The Richard Dawkins Collection.

- Eckman P., (1996) In the Footsteps of the Yellow Emperor, Cypress Book Company, San Francisco.

- Fruehauf H., (1999), Science, Politics, and the making of "TCM": Chinese Medicine in Crisis, Journal of Chinese Medicine, Number 61 Oct. 1999, JCM Publications, Hove, England.

- Fukuoka M., (1992), One-Straw Revolution: Introduction to Natural Farming, Other India Press, Goa, India.

- Fukushima K., (1999) Meridian Therapy: A hands-on text on Traditional Hari Based on Pulse Diagnosis; Third edition, Toyo Hari Medical Association, Tokyo.

- (DVD): Harding D. E, (2006) On Having No Head: Seeing One's Original Nature, The Shollond Trust.

- Harding D.E., (1952) The Hierarchy of Heaven and Earth, Faber and Faber

- Harding D. E (1961) On Having No Head: Zen and the rediscovery of the obvious, The Shollond Trust.

- Harding D. E (2001) The Science of the 1st Person: Its Principles , Practice and Potential, The Sholland Trust.

- Harvey C. & S., (1999), Principles of Astrology, Thorsons-HarperCollins Publishers, Hammersmith, London.

- Ikeda M., (2005), The Practice of Japanese Acupuncture and Moxibustion: Classic Principles in Action, Eastland Press, Seattle.

- Kishi, A. and Whieldon, A., (2011). Sei-ki: Life in Resonance, The secret art of Shiatsu, London, UK, Singing Dragon.

- Kuwahara K., (2003), Traditional Japanese Acupuncture: Fundamentals of Meridian Therapy: The Society of Traditional Japanese Medicine, Complementary Medicine Press, Taos, New Mexico.

- Krishnamurti U.G, (2002), Mind is Myth, Smriti Books. ISBN: 8187967102

- Lad V., (2004) Ayurveda: The science of Self-healing, Lotus Press, Wisconsin.

- Lau D.C., (1964), Lao Tzu: Tao Te Ching, Penguin Books Inc., Middlesex, England.

- Lovelock J., (2010), BBC4 documentary: Beautiful Minds, part 2: James Lovelock (19th April 2010)

- Masunaga S. (1987), Meridian Exercises, Japan Publications , Tokyo.

- Matsumoto K., Birch S (1983), Five Elements and Ten Stems, Paradigm Publications, Brookline.

- Matsumoto K., Birch S (1988), Hara Diagnosis: Reflections on the Sea, Paradigm Publications, Brookline

- (DVD): Mctaggart L., Liptom B., Pearl E., (2009), The Living Matrix.

- (DVD): Mctaggart L., (2007) Biology of Transformation (DVD set of 6) - A Living The Field conference.

- Mctaggart L., (2008), The Field: The Quest for the Secret Force of the Universe, Harper

- Nightingale F., (1859), Notes on Nursing: what it is and what it is not, Dover Publications Inc.

- Parsons T., (1995), The Open Secret, Open Secret Publishing, Dorset , UK.

- Parsons T., (2000), As It Is: Dialogues on The Open Secret, Dorset , UK.

- Pearl E., (2001), The Reconnection: Heal Others, Heal Yourself, Hay House.

- Rapgay L., (1996),The Tibetan Book of Healing, Lotus Press, Wisconsin.

- Spencer H., (2009), The Principles of Biology, Cornell University Library.

- Wilhelm R., (1968), I Ching or Book of changes, Penguin Books, London

- Wittgenstein L., (1921) Tractatus Logico-Philosophicus, 2 edition, Routledge

- Wu N.L and Wu A.Q., (1997), Yellow Emperor's Canon Internal Medicine, China Science & Technology Press.

Internet resources

- Stevenson M., (1932) Footprints, http://www.wowzone.com/fprints.htm

- Permaculture quotes Bill Mellison, Masanobu Fukuoka from:- http://www.permacultureplanet.com/

- Greek medicine: http://www.greekmedicine.net/b_p/Four_basic_qualities.html

- Muir J., (1901) Quote from "Our National Parks" by http://en.wikiquote.org/wiki/John_Muir

- Einstein Quote from:- http://www.einstein-quotes.com/ThinkingKnowledge.html

- New Testament quote from:- http://bible.cc/mark/12-31.html

- A Speech by Chief Seattle of the Dwamish Tribe in 1854, http://www.rainbowbody.net/ongwhehonwhe/chiefsea.html

- Guinness World records for strange diets: http://www.guinnessworldrecords.com/records/amazing_feats/unusual_skills/strangest_diet.aspx

medical oneness

www.ingramcontent.com/pod-product-compliance
Lightning Source LLC
Chambersburg PA
CBHW031933190326
41519CB00007B/515